55
Golden Pieces

55 Golden Pieces

All illustrations by the Haitian artist Patrick Gaspard.

ISBN: 979-8-9904918-0-9 (hardcover)
         979-8-9904918-1-6 (paperback)
         979-8-9904918-2-3 (ebook)

Printed in the United States of America

55
Golden
Pieces

Jean René Bazin PierrePierre

Table des matières

Foreword

-I am the younger brother
And I remember one instance when my brother defended me against a
bully. And he would have done it everytime, but I became big enough
to fight my own battles. My brother requested of me what I consider a
challenging task, that of writing a short preamble to his book. With no
prediction, I discovered a poet in the English language with an insight
in poetry coupled with elegant rhyming skills. Oh, there is much more
to my brother than that. On the outside looking in, I also remember
a young adonis of a brother, appreciated by his friends and loved by
women, fine dancer and big fan of "les Shleu-Shleu". That same brother
who, one fine morning, turned out to be a "disciple" that Victor Hugo
would have knighted. That kindness and strength of character, clashing
with the rawness of certain writings. I greatly appreciate a writer
who doesn't hide behind his art to become irresponsible. A writer who,
rather that shocking and giving you goosebumps, inspires you to elevate
your heart and soul towards the Source of it all, the divine Love…
I cordially invite you to discover what my dear brother has to offer.
I hope you enjoy the read.

—Maxime Bazin PierrePierre

Preface

…Therefore inspiration, the work of the Spirit,
Will always reach the ones that it wants to nourish.
Lovingly, stealthily, it leads to the finish
The soul that once chosen, opens up to its treats .

There's never a recess, nor a lack of resource
Since it draws directly all from the divine font.
It glides over heartaches, all miseries affront,
Comes amid any toil, tramples plans on their course.

It flies over frontiers, shuns genders and all race,
Has no times at its clock, never rings any bell.
It shows no preference, any gloom it can quell,
Though rare and much precious, when sought for leaves no trace.

It enlightens us all, ignorant and unread,
Gives places of honor amid dignitaries.
And the load is so light that it asks to carry
That it weighs like feather, and feels light as a thread.

Therefore inspiration, sensing humility,
Will come and crash ashore of the many chosen.
Never has it been said that they were left frozen,
Those who so stealthily receive its verity.

Recall

The supple timbre of your voice
That the silence comes in to chase
Rings on my mind like a sweet noise
And tills the landscape of my face.

Once upon it was melody
That the most skillful of cellist
With golden fingers though sturdy
Would one day ever find the piste.

Once upon at its very sound
As sweet and sassy as can be,
Any worry that was around
Would surely be matched, not maybe.

The supple timbre of your voice
That in my heart left a deep trace
Comes often to make me rejoice
As you come bask in my embrace.

Often life brings its tragedies
Then I'm submerged by daily deeds
But amid all these maladies
Its solace always comes to feed.

There I rejoin the quiescence
That foments the recall of words,
These words uttered for sustainance
For now I live on what's once heard.

The supple timbre of your voice
Will always remain audible,
And stamp my world with content poise
Though now you are unreachable.

But as you're now so far away,
Now that my whole world imploded,
Now that the silence got its way,
All your words my mind downloaded.

And they resound to ease my pain,
They resound like a good old seed
That planted deep within my brain
Gives solace as they slowly feed.

The suppple timbre of your voice
Showers my world with words that fit.
They know they are my unique choice,
They know they are my loving treat.

They come at the rise of the sun
They entertain my loneliness,
They linger as bearer of fun
Till the moon the earth come caress.

And so it went, and so it goes
While my life carries the remnants,
The remnants of love that echoes
And just won't die while I lament.

The supple timbre of your voice
Declares out loud my love for you.
It attests that there's no more choice,
That I'll be yours my whole life through.

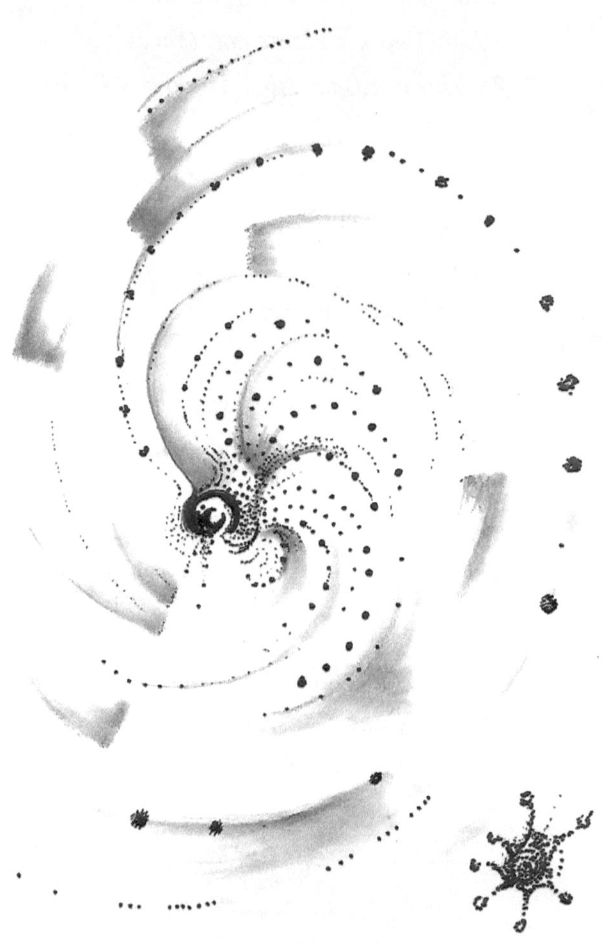

Suddenly

Suddenly, in life it nudges
Just ignoring one's surroundings,
Suddenly, appeasing grudges,
Love in our hearts makes a landing.

Suddenly now we are speechless,
Suddenly hung to a bright smile.
Suddenly, it is so priceless,
Suddenly it was worth the while

That we waited so long to see
These eyes in which our sun rises,
This face revealing God's mercy,
As if His mercy had sizes.

But suddenly the elation,
The heart racing, the sweaty palms,
The dry mouth, verbal confusion,
Love has landed with its sweet balm.

Suddenly, like no déjà vu,
She is the queen of your palace,
Suddenly, right in your purview,
All your plans you gladly replace.

Sorrow street

In this small house of Sorrow street,
Around the table we all sit,
Gathered to have our dinner treats,
My dear sister, but you are gone.
The pain lingers in every heart
Since that day you chose to depart,
That grief in us planted its dart,
Of your kind words now we hear none.

Why did you have to go so soon?
You had our love, O dearest boon,
We no longer can hear you croon,
For sadly with us you're not there.
The pain that you so long carried,
You stoically never varied,
You always gay, always merry,
To everyone showed tender care.

You gladly chose our parents stance.
Sadly we did not stand a chance,
Over us they had preference,
So you crossed to their side of shore.
In Sorrow street, that house so bleak,
Your presence everywhere yet sticks,
Your soothing words everyone seeks,
Their sounds lull us deep in the core.

The kids took a damaging blow,
The best auntie they had to show,
All crushed under debris below.
O my sister, what an anguish!
And suddenly what emptiness!
What heavy load on every chest!
Each one silently does his best
But we all miss the so cherished.

Thalie will move on. She is strong.
She carries well her sorrow prongs.
Well imbued of what's right or wrong
She'll go forward as half orphan.
May the good Lord show clemency,
And enfold you in His mercy
So to relieve our poignancy.
To Him all pray'rs and shows of hands.

Clearwater Beach Pier

(Summer Eve)

The crimson sky of late July
In the air puts an eerie touch.
You see late birds here and there fly
To finish errands in a rush.

Relentless waves with foamy crowns
Come crashing gainst the wooden pier
Whose moldy beams don't give a frown;
Their shoving, they no longer fear.

The golden sand now dark and gray
Still retains traces of the crowd.
The many bodies that here lay
Left echoes that are much too loud.

There you can see the tall hotel
Hugging its frontal part of sand.
There a small crowd tries not to quell
The noise of their half naked band.

A few lovers go hand in hand
With feet in the foamy waters.
While happy tods dance to the band
Whose rhythm they seem to falter.

The palm trees welcome the cooling
Now that the sun is far away.
They stand erect, so imposing,
Standing its heat day after day.

The merchants gathered on the pier
Begin repacking unsold goods
While others profit of the mere
Occasions to open their hoods.

The ice cream parlor's still open
To young girls and their families,
And young boys who return often
To skateboard while keeping tallies.

The sea birds you no longer see
Took part at this afternoon feast.
They ate, swooping with no mercy,
Of human beings afraid the least.

And patiently, and patiently
The fishermen hold to their bait.
They hang as on a balcony,
Pond'ring over their dinner fate.

But often their concentration
Is broken by the quick surging
Of a jet sky strong pulsation
To its dock safely returning.

If suddenly you hear a scream,
Sign of random successful catch,
It gives the rest of them, it seems,
Some hope for a much longer watch.

The band had long taken a break.
The surf's now roaring loud and clear.
A little girl cries her heartache,
From the water she was too near.

So in the arms of her mother
She gesticulates a tantrum.
Before I could see her laughter
Now I see the frown of her mum.

Those two remaining on the sand
Seem to ignore the passers-by.
They don't see those they may offend,
They don't, while on the sand they lie.

And suddenly you get to see
The lights of Tampa Bay by night
Glittering the indigo sea,
A genuine delight to the sight.

Closer to me a proud old man
Displays his catch of the evening,
A feisty trout whose dinner plan
Just became the old man's feeding.

And the band resumes its vacarm,
And the crowd their dirty dancing.
And this young lady full of charm
Can't even hear her cellphone ring.

A rugged young man is upset
At the gate keeper of the pier,
The change he put just could not get
To work the turnstile, it appears.

So louder, longer they argue
Till finally some other guy
Offers the quarter overdue
For him who hurriedly zooms by

Rushing to the end of the pier
Bringing to his other pana
What could as well have been a beer,
Forbidden on the marina.

And the darkness made its entrance
Robed in a gown of shiny stars,
By then the crowd got in a transe
Caused by the "Island Superstars".

And so it came, and so it went
This Saturday of late July.
A few teens came folding the tents,
Helping this older, skinnier guy.

What then to do, what, tell me please,
What else to savor, the weather?
Seventy-nine lovely degrees,
A gorgeous evening, my brother!

Sweet nothings

Oh my lovely baby,
Oh how I think of thee!
Thine eyes, my horizon
Provoke my confusion.
Truly I have never
Experience such rapture.
If ever of thy world
To me thou don't unfurl
I'll remain poor, lonely,
All withered and weary.
Conversely if instead
My heart thou hold with stead,
I will sing happily
And worship thou solely.

The pier and I

The shade of sand, the rank of fish
Overtly lurking in the air,
Amid July nonchalant pairs
Showcasing their cheap love affairs
In this landscape they so cherish.

Alone in the midst of my sighs
Let me decline the lucid thoughts
Raking my soul while I'm still caught
In this lament that I long fought,
But like the tide, is now knee high.

Had it not been for you

Had it not been for you, through the thick and the thin,
Through my every season: spring, summer, winter, fall,
Had it not been for you, the voice of every call,
Will I be standing here with all this love within?

Had it not been for you, from the very get go,
Who polished the image of my deep wounded soul,
Who rekindled that flame of love story of old
And fine-tuned my poor heart to yours steady echo?

Had it not been for you, with shoulder wet from tears,
Tears shed through the seasons, the friends, the boos, the wives,
Disheartening failures, gut-wrenching inner strives,
Would there be this angel to chase away my fears?

Had it not been for you, the hero of my dreams,
Who quenched all my fires set up by all the foes,
Who dispelled the distress of my slighted ego,
Would there be a soul mate to silence all my screams?

But it's been only you, my love, my angel fine,
My faithful companion, my well-hidden treasure,
My source of love divine, the dew of my nature.
It's only for your love that from now on I pine.

The Sun

Do you know, my lady
Why the early morning
To your face peacefully
Gentle smile seems to bring?

The sun, my blessed child,
With rays spreading galore,
Springs from the undefiled
The thought of love once more.

So placidly spurning
The nightly escapades,
Receive its rays blessings.
Don't linger in the shade.

For the sun, my darling,
With brightness or pallor,
To your soul always brings
Love from your Creator.

Mercy, Lord

When I am alone and sad
And around me the world's gone mad.
When I feel I will not make
The many plans I undertake.

If I feel too big my pride
Though my sorrow I cannot hide.
When the pain is much to bear,
Not even a smile I can wear.

When I try to make amend
For your sweet Face I did offend
For I failed to land a hand
At my neighbor's pressing demand.

And if I kneel down and pray,
From my cry Lord, don't turn away.
I will wait, O my Savior,
Your forgiveness will not falter.

Wild thinking

I see it irks listening
To my rants with line so bleak
And the words of my rhyming
Though you know well what they seek
Fail to nudge your stark thinking.

Never has it been a trend
Living in these nowadays
With all mores that this world bends
To ask that the human prays,
Fear of neighbors to offend.

What I now hold in esteem
To my mate is obsolete
I just cannot make it seem
Upholding what she sees fit
To be pursued as a dream.

I'll never, I know I tried,
To change or dilute the truth,
Make believe or just plain lie
See the slaughtering of sooth
And calmly keep a blind eye.

Whoever gospel contorts
Either for pride or just greed
Or afraid of clear retort
So from their conscience to speed
In detrimental effort

Is bound to bawl and grind teeth
Left stranded in sheer mire
For no teaching should one sieve
Holy Ghost not to tire
And thus the brethren deceive.

Away from me then depart
And go hang out with hip crowds.
They do not follow their heart
But rather feel very proud
Of their most vile inner parts.

Crosses are sown all over
When carried you get merits
Needed for safe crossover
As combo soul and spirit
Sheds off their carnal cover.

The world tends to become one
The borders slowly fading
Alllegiance they claim to none
Everyone who's suffering
Has crown of thorns and a throne.

Meanwhile deep, deep within me
I guard safely the strong hope
Fueling dreams ever stormy
That they clash and fail to cope
With Heavens pink and balmy.

Therefore what I say I say
As I throw my net to sea
I will have yea or have nay
But I pray one day you see
That as I write so I pray.

You'll go clamor word misuse
Look for ways to shut me down
The semantics I abuse
Come trickling down from the frown
Of the one I call my muse.

First poem to Junie, 1/28/1997

My Darling

Just wanted to tell you how sweet your embrace feels
And how holding you close marveled me to the chills.
The magic of the Bay, the sweet peace of your room
Made that last Sunday night ecstatic, free of gloom.

I had to be away from what I so treasure
To swear not to ever refrain from such pleasure.
You made me feel so new, so warm and so alive
That I declare aloud that you're my better half.

I love you my darling, and for so strong reasons
That I often wonder why do I stay alone.
But to rush is to fail, nothing is finalized
Unless it is over and over analyzed.

So darling, we'll get there though again we may face
Either tougher rival or even bigger mace.
Enough, I said enough, let me just end my rhyme
With the sweet taste I have of getting back my prime.

No more stumble

For the very first day you crashed into my life
You magically just quelled my every single strife.
I followed you blindly,
And loved you so kindly
That in a quite short time you had become my wife.

But soon I discovered that you were but a fake
For from you I received nothing but sheer heartache.
Nothing lasts for ever,
But I swore to never
Go again and repeat such a foolish mistake.

Life with us plays its game but often what we get
Marks us deep in the core, and we just can't forget,
For taken so aback
We get shoved off our track,
Bruised up and sore as though we were wounded target.

I invested my all, never thought you'd fail me.
You promised everything to the trusting dummy
Wrapped around your finger.
You became the stinger
And my heart fell stricken under this infamy.

But for the life of me, I swore you were the one
You did everything right, not an act was undone.
You knew all the right moves
My perturbed mind to soothe
Until the wretched time when feelings you had none.

We tried all kind of help, you went along with it,
Blaming it all on stress, you so shrewd and so fit
When your coldness swan dove
It came my heart to shove
And right between our souls, calmly it took a seat.

I remembered your words, recalled all your gestures
Which made it all tougher your new stance to endure
But at every clear dawn
Like a baffled, sad pawn,
Pitifully I'd hope for some brighter future.

But the years came and went, but nothing in you changed,
You simply left my world, grew steadily estranged.
We ceased to be a pair,
For this ill love affair
Had retired your smile and all plans rearranged.

So life for us went on, each one living his own.
I had nowhere to go since my heart you disowned,
But you followed your plan,
Knew quite well where to stand,
You stood there for sometimes, glowing in the unknown.

But through all I carried from your bold change of heart
The worst showed up after, tore mine into small parts.
Never saw it coming,
But you went on wiling,
It was a risk taken by the ones way too smart.

Twas blow below the belt but it was your best shot,
It hit in broad daylight, got me so much distraught
That even your close friends
Stepped in to put an end
To what they all saw as something no one would sought.

When I look at it now, now that it's all behind,
I somewhat feel releived but it dwells on my mind
That one can never tell
They know any one well.
Brace yourself for the worst, but in all remain kind.

To any one who'd ask, I'd answer them the same,
That's what life's all about, that no one is to blame,
That in spite of all this,
That some call cowardice,
I won't harbor hatred or behaving with shame.

For early I was taught that whatever you sow,
Acts of gentle kindness or deceit in a row
Before it is too late,
You receive on your plate
The same vibes you sent out with gloomy greif in tow.

Whereas what is suffered in blessed tolerance,
In turn pours over you your share of recompense,
In bundle as He says,
On your laps it will lay
For the whole world to see, and they won't call it chance.

For losers of this world are never true losers.
They appear as failures compared to the others,
But what they seem to lack
One day will swing right back,
And all over their world sow blessings in showers.

Oh yes you left and went your bright and merry way,
Yes I stayed there choking on all that I could say.
I bid you true farewell,
It's all that I could tell
Though deep inside I wish you would not go away.

But the fate that befalls the average human being
Comes swiftly upon him, his plans, readjusting.
It bursts one sunny day,
Spreads its load of dismay,
Rearranging his world with no hint, no warning.

The turmoil that ensues is never déjà vu.
It comes with a program and knows well its purview.
It comes lessons to teach,
It comes stressing on each
And every blunt aspect, spreading grief and sinew.

The subject it ensnares will always resurface
In the world he resides with a rose or a mace.
A rose, to spread more love,
Mace, with hatred to shove
Every one around him and with bitterness lace.

Stressors in this here life bring out of us the best.
The true self will emerge revealing the deep chest.
The bitter one will rage,
The meek one will be sage.
This always takes effect at the end of all tests.

But always from above is given the free will,
The will to please the light or pamper hatred still.
Regardless of the blow,
Regardless of how low,
What you give in return, your true nature reveals.

Misery well carried brings about blessed things.
When mishandled it pours calamities in strings.
It's the offered solace
To the ones who truce chase
When despite all efforts only pure grief life brings.

And they press on knowing that better days will come,
And they press on hoping on the blessed Kingdom
That will arrive for sure
For it is well ensured
By the One whose Spirit enlightens, the Awesome.

And yet in spite of all life keeps its steady course.
Regardless of failures do not craddle remorse.
A clean slate is offered
To the soul who suffered
And can offer his pain for some spiritual bourse.

This trade is feasible at just every level
For the soul always gains when the body snivels.
It rises and ascends
And joyfully transcends,
Nearing hidden treasures to its sight unravel.

But we pamper one self, stepping on everyone.
Despite the "Thou shall not" no one spares any one.
The world karma's tarnished.
True love has long vanished
From every human heart where it once gladly shone.

Everyone claims the right to bear their deepest stains
Right out on their sleeve, to their neighbor's expense.
Everything is allowed,
Everything is avowed
And all this just baffles even the common sense.

So went my reflexion, all alone in the dark,
As I drown in sorrow on this stage grim and stark.
All the wisdom you gained
Failed to help you retain
The peace within your soul that now left a sad mark.

If I survive this blow, the Spirit is able,
I will not once again suffer such a stumble.
Life to us can be kind
But yet we ought to mind
The stones on this journey. The heart's no more nimble.

I'll take my load of grief as it was sent to me
But for now will steer clear of any infamy.
Though crushed and downtrodden
I will stay in this den,
Will not go entertain any kind of gamy.

But yes, when I saw her, I thought of lucky star,
But little did I know I had found one that chars.
Now all scorched up I stand,
But now I understand
No more stumble for me, I have my share of scars.

Baby

If I could reach out to you
And hold you in my arms anew,
Feel your heart beating against mine
And let you know it will be fine,
That from this world of misery
Nothing will stop me.

I'd satisfy all your demands,
Would take your head into my hands,
And from the look in your brown eyes
Would recognize my precious prize.
I'd reveal my secrets to you,
Tell me, tell me what would you do?...

I'd kiss your eyes, sing you to sleep,
Step right in to your dreams so deep.
Then together in our dreamland
We'd walk happily hand in hand.
Your voice like a sweet lullaby
Would turn from gray our clear blue sky.

We'd go far away
Seal our love that day,
Lovingly I'd hear you say
Here's my heart
But this time to keep,
Here's my heart to keep.
If I would give my heart to you
Tell me baby, what would you do?

Ghost of fall

Spirit of fall, Autumn leaves cover your demise,
To infuse in all our hearts blessed hope.
Ghost, mournful to the eyes,
Convey to us all
Pledges of the fall.

Spirit of fall, enchant us with your magic shades,
To enliven the world, your vast domain,
Caught in your leaf parade
Sustain deep within us
A sense of trust.

I offer you tears of all broken hearts,
All sufferings muffled by your leaves,
I bring to you all lovers torn apart,
Walking your streets, hearts upon sleeves.

Here at your feet, I commit my sorrow,
The joys of old, all hopes deeply fondled.
Winter awaits, ghost of fall will you blow
Far, far away all pain carried in bundle.

Let Her Know

If ever
You'd prefer
To possess any other,
Remember
You told her
She's the loveliest flower.
If one day
She should say
That she wants to go away
Cause you may
Have betray'
Her and left her in dismay.

Then again
My dear friend
Tell her : "Come and take my hand",
Don't pretend
That you can
Make it alone till the end.
Then only
Your chérie
Will always be yours solely
And gently
You and she
Will drift to eternity.

Let her know
That she's the one,
That you are
Nothing without her,
That you'd die
If she were gone,
That you would
Give your life for her.
Let her know
That she's the one.

With a gift

With all the love for a lady
Come this token on Christmas eve,
Just to reveal to her clearly
My heart resting upon my sleeve.

So please, receive this little charm,
Petty proof of my love for you.
Let it gently your spirit warm
And remain with you all life through.

The Angels

They're here and there, they're everywhere
They walk or they fly in the air,
They're busy dealing God's affairs
But never tire.

They have no gender, have no race,
They come to us but leave no trace
They assume any shape or face,
Any attire.

But anyone they come to nudge
With nimble pace or draggy trudge
Always attests feeling love surge
From within their soul

For whenever they come to us,
It's always to bring a surplus
Of tender care needed and thus
Sent to make us whole.

When suddenly from out of nought
The many plans we have unwrought
Come through by someone whom we thought
Would never assist.

When in the heart love comes to stir
The many dreams we chase after
To magically all gloom deter
Moping to desist,

And when we fall so easy prey
Of the flesh snares how hard we pray
And lose all blessing sent our way
And we lose all hope

Then shows up, in God's urgency,
Someone we thought we'd never see,
Revealing the Father's mercy,
Precious divine dope.

When despite all the faith instilled
We come to doubt the Lord's Love still
Although our heart His Spirit fills
Giving us His life

And we drift away from His grace
Lost in this everyday rat race
That chars the soul, furrows the face,
Cuts deep like a knife.

They come then swiftly, by God sent,
They come to help us all repent,
They come down in swooping descent
Our ills to expel

They come and bring us His solace
They come with enfolding embrace
They come bringing to us God's grace,,
They are the Angels.

I Am Sorry

I really think I should
Explain my attitude.
I was cold as you said,
You felt low, felt betrayed.

But before you condemn
And ask me for your claim,
You should be fair and just
And let me explain first.

The last time that you and I met
In control I watch you go down.
But deep inside of me I felt
So bad, but you saw not my frown.

Loving Darling, is a feeling,
That takes you high as a ceiling.
But to this coin there's flip side
By suffering you must abide.

I felt so hurt, felt it so deep,
Found it hard my composure to keep.
Almost made a fool of myself,
Felt like putting love back on shelf.

Bear with me baby, be patient.
At this I declare I'm novice.
Never have I felt love like this,
Of my swings, please be tolerant.

I'll try next time to keep my cool
And of myself not make a fool.
I'll remember that, as they say,
Good things do come to those who pray.

And if ever such happening
To your loving eyes tears should bring,
I promise I will make amend
And never again will offend.

I write

The world is now nearing its end
Whispers in my ears a close friend.
See the sun shines not as before
The sea waves swell and loudly roar.
The clouds are hanging much lower
The air we breathe is heavier
But I ignore all these, and write.
Peacefully relaxing, I write,
Through all my hopes and fears, I write
And I give thanks.

The neighbors lost their cat again
It took off after the last rain
But the couple blames the mail man,
Who this jam really can't amend.
They finally opened the road
The one that last year no one rode
But I don't leave the desk, I write,
All through my nights and days, I write,
When all is said and done, I write
And I am grateful.

Chinese's spoken more than English,
No one got that there was a glitch
And Africa is split in two,
Wonder whose dream this made come true,
And they discovered a new moon,
The whole world will visit it soon
But I just keep my stance and write,
With all sand in my eyes, I write,
Choosing pen or keyboard, I write,
And I give praise.

And the pollen wreaks its havoc,
Hot summer days begin to knock
The indian ocean is all dry,
In it fell a large load of rye,
And all sea fruits got sick of it,
They swam fast but found no exit,
So like them in my den I write,
No escape, no recess, I write
Fed of the same manna, I write
And I delight.

My Lovely Little Bird

O my baby Erie,
My sweet little chérie
You came breathe life in me,
You teach my heart to sing the loveliest of symphony,
You took it for a spin with your angelic voice,
You kiss my breath away to forever-spring land.

The melodious sound
Of the tone of your words
Reminds me that I found
A pearl from all these herds.

The glow of your brown eyes
Reveals me free of lies
That heaven does exist.
I can never resist
The softness of your hands
But no one understands
Why it's you
Again you
Always you
You, you, you.

I live in slow motion each time
Of your voice I don't hear the chime.
My world remains a mere shadow
Till you step in it tomorrow.

Then just as suddenly
My joy comes back again
Cause baby, you have me
In the palm of your hand.

Like a flower

Like a flower you come adorn
The bleak and somber world of mine.
By the others it has been scorned
But you came and it gladly shines.

Like a flower you come dispense
Your aroma of love and care
That trickles and changes this tense
And stressy landscape all so bare.

Your jokes and laughter then recoil
Stroking the walls of my chamber
Where quietly I char and toil
With my psyche calm yet somber.

Like a flower sprinkle your dew
Over the dryness of my land
My parched lips tremble as we two
Cuddle, cuddle in loving trend.

Like a flower therefore remain
With bright petals and long, slim stalk.
Be my angel, I'll be your man
And freely we'll let our hearts talk.

What Is This

From the many blows I received
To all the lovers I deceived,
The love that for you my heart bears
Favors pure celestial affairs.

Who would have thought that in a glance
We'd be caught in this jolly dance?
When in the rapture of this bliss,
I humbly wonder: "What is this?"
My soul amid all this frenzy
Reminds my tipsy heart softly:

"Love is the quintessential gift
That mercifully is bequeathed"
To the ones who through sufferings"
From the Lord still expect all things."

"Therefore don't think your heart's at stakes"
When lovingly your hand she takes."
You just received from God above"
His bléssed and once-pomised love."

Sketching

I sit alone amid the sound
Of thoughts running wild on my mind
They run like kids on open ground,
Run leaving my hearbeats behind.

They run pass the cemetery
Where lie slaughtered the dreams we made
They run afraid of the eerie
Glow emerging from the tomb shades.

Lack of vigor or lack of zest
I just don't feel up to the chase.
They drown the beating in my chest
For you age as you stay in place.

But then now come unknown faces
Some come smiling, some rather not
They fly living shadow traces,
They fly for they see me distraught.

Then I contemplate better days
Where nightingales would come along
To make amend for my dismay,
Bring solace needed for so long.

All compell me to write and write
So I can dispel this mistruth.
As Sunday to the week is light
As clear hope is to blessed truth.

But let it be, just let it be,
Let it on my mind wreak havoc.
Give my wackineess this freebie,
To my thoughts don't put any block.

Long, long ago I had a plan,
A plan solid as a refrain
But when in me this came to land
Pure ravage beset my poor brain

Which for a while went on idling
Leaving my body vegetate
While the whole world went on living
Moved by my being and its state.

Then I return to my tableau
Well aware of what is at stake,
So not to interrupt the flow
Of these thoughts coming loose but fake.

Always when carrying a cross
Willfully one forsakes the rest
And on the road where grows no moss
All flowers have long lost their zest.

But love in the midst of it all
In its splendor blots every flaw.
From all tree tops you hear the calls
Of white doves with roses in claw.

What is offered to me as balm
Never had any worth in pence.
It has been the cheapest of palms
For those deprived of common sense.

This chaos that seems to bring peace
Rings in my ears rendered now deaf.
But my mind still fails to dismiss
This havoc that has never left.

But breathe and breathe, expell the heat
Caused by this damage of psyche.
Bring down, bring down your rate of beats,
This heart witnessed scenes too freaky.

And every time comes a new song
Deemed to upset my inner peace
It comes ringing so vile and strong
That each dawn I hope this would cease.

But the sun with its heat persists
Leaning heavy gainst the windows
So bright that shadows lose their pistes
And run hide into deep furrows.

But as I lose my sanity
Wrapped in folds of my common sense
What I spit in audacity
I used to call it pure nonsense.

Meanwhile alone I sit and watch
Faces, shadows and deafening sounds,
As they descend, a scary batch
Set to distabilized my ground.

Lack of vigor or lack of zest,
Soon all this will have a meaning.
I'll focus on passing the test
That so far has kept me dreaming.

Sing Alleluia

Give thanks, give thanks to Him, our Lord.
He gives what we can't afford.
His love for us knows no boundary,
He longs to show us His Mercy.

So many times we hear His call
But many times we fail and fall,
But He, the merciful Father,
Forgets His creatures but never.

He gives us his mighty Spirit
Which our poor nature does complete.
Throughout our life He sustains us
That in His eyes we remain just.

He repeatedly when we pray
Strenghtens us in all our dismay,
And lovingly stands us steady
Amid our own sin misery.

So many times He gives us sight
Of his great Love, Power and Might
But senselessly we come up short
Of His truth we often contort.

So now sing praises to our God.
Give thanks to the Almighty Lord.
Towards us He shows His kindness
And gives us lots of His richness.

Then make a testimony leap
For if a king's treasure's to keep
The work of God we should declare,
With the whole world His graces share.

My lucky star

Rolling stone with no moss,
Heading straight for my loss,
Tossed around here and there as the wind blows.
I'd go from ecstasy
To darkened misery
But one day in my eyes I saw a glow
It was you, my lucky star.

Twas a dim yet steady gleam high above my pit
But it shone so steadily,
Shone so merrily,
And from this instance if I am back on my feet,
It's cause I have your soft light
Always there in my sight.

You enliven my world,
You glitter like a pearl,
And you sing lovingly through every chore.
And like the dearest prize
I set on you my eyes,
And I'm happy unlike ever before
Following my lucky star.

Now I rest so peacefully all through the seasons
Clinching deep within my soul
What now makes me whole,
And when they come inquire, I hide the reason
Why the glow of your soft light
Makes my world gay and bright.

Caspar

To You

I stand before you knocking at your door,
I stand before you as I did before,
I stand before you, all naked and poor
With only my love sung as an encore.

Repeatedly I hear: "Go your own way!"
I'm living my life, find yours in the hay".
You left it down there acting so foolish,"
Be a man for once, it's over, finished."

But here I still stand like a lonely dog
All afraid to go facing this thick fog.
I have one mistress, a lovely lady,
How can I ever exist or be me
If she does not hold secure of my leash,
I surely one day, get lost and perish.

O chérie, I beg, listen to my plea,
It's again the voice of your poor baby
Coming back to life from his misery
And praying out loud for you to marry.

Chérie if ever I had another,
Never but never would they make waver
My heart beating strong but for you only
Which if in your hands would be so merry.

I can't my baby, I can't forget you.
God knows how I tried, tried to start anew,
But your face, my love, so sweet in my hands,
Eclipse all others who between us stand.
I will forever beg for your pardon
And don't ask me why or for what reasons
You should to my plea give your attention
I'd gladly answer —no hesitation —
Listen to your heart for there still resides
The love for me you so hard try to hide…

Marijune

I smell your light-scented fragrance,
The autumn leaves gently bowing,
The trees branches slowly wagging.
You're back to me as blesséd chance
As I always knew you'd return,
You for whom my heart always yearn,

Marijune, come rest your weary feet.
Come into my arms, you need not to greet.
All has been said from soul to soul,
We both have paid this heavy toll.

Marijune, all miseries now leave behind,
Grab a hold of what Heavens help us find.
Marijune smile now for my eyes to see,
The glow in your sight attests God's mercy.

Come into my arms, your soul come restore,
Come, don't shed a tear, come claim this encore.
Come regain your throne, come shine as before,
Come reign on my world. Come, to bliss we'll soar.

To You (end)

…I often picture this blesséd evening
When my eyes on you will do I landing.
The stars in the sky will surely rejoice
And in their own way will second your choice.
This world will remain a sorowful place,
It will rain sometimes, the moon won't change face.
The sun will always warms us with its rays
But even among this known disarray,
I know with your love, my world will be kind
For the sole reason that you're on my mind.

If only you knew how much I cherish
The fall when it puts on leaves its finish.
This just reminds me of you my baby,
See how much I learnt from you, my Junie.

I'll try not to bore you any longer.
Though I spilled my guts like any other
I hope that within your heart you still have
The strength you once had to show me the path
Back into your arms, for there I desire,
Comes rain or comes shine, to live the entire
Rest of this ordeal that you call my life,
Hoping that safe there, I'll settle my strife.

I stand before you knocking at your door,
I stand before you like never before.
I stand before you with my heart still sore,
I stand before you baby, hear my score.

Rhyming

Though it so much tickles the ears
Rhyming just does not make a poem.
But if away from it you steer
Your wave will crash without a foam.

Thus rhyming is to your reader
The icing on his tasty cake.
The whole desert is much sweeter,
Enhancing the dough you just bake'.

The choice of rhyme doesn't matter
As much as how it does surprise
The reader who comes take shelter
Within the lines they render wise.

Often it shows the skillfulness
And the writer's inspiration,
Showing that they have more or less
Used wit and imagination.

It is given high importance
In certain school of great poetry
But in some much modern romance
The stress is placed on the sultry.

But as it's in the classic case,
One swims in the sea of one's choice.
The clever bird will show its face
Only to a familiar voice.

One can never pull from a hat
The rabbit they never possess'
But if they pulled many – so what,
Let your ears enjoy the caress.

Their Plight

Now that it came to your backyard
As it did for so many times,
Now that it made you feel awkward
You ask me to jot a few rhymes

On the riveting videos
Passed around all over the net.
They smacked your Haitian ego
Or your human heart, they upset.

But if they offend the public
It's just that the cellphone era
Renders the news much too epic
Hence the dark clouds on your aura.

But I assure you my dear friend,
Though upsetting, 'tis no big deal.
The world down to its very end
Will stage these atrocities still.

The human being has deep inside
This well-rooted dark tendency
To crush the weak ones at their side
Who stand as a minority.

See the plight of the Israelites
Pulled from the snares of the Pharaoh
And that of the africanites
From the slaves and now the ghettos.

Remembers well the genocides
For reasons that reason ignores,
Done repeatedly, done with pride,
Done with furor the world abhors.

The other one always delights
Each and every time he succeeds
At cashing on the human plight,
Use it, his darkest self to feed.

Yes, it's shocking and appalling
To see the dark one in action
But what kills you seeing these scenes
Is not the mere situation

But rather the fact that you saw
What otherwise you'd only hear.
It leaves a long sounding echo
That away from you just won't steer.

But Earth despite its nastiness
Will stay on her trajectory
As long as humans are possess'
They'll feed their beasts in a hurry.

My love for you

The love of you keeps me alive,
Giving me my every day drive.
The love of you keeps me ensnared
Right in the dungeon of your heart,
Your heart that's needed to jump start
My heart stalling without your care.

The love of you gives me strong wings
To bear my lot of sufferings,
Those which describe my state of mind,
My mind where your name wreaks havoc,
Though it's I who live on to stalk
The souvenirs you left behind.

The love of you I so cherish
Saddles me like some strong hashish.
There, all I see are your brown eyes,
That shine as pair of guiding lights.
And I, the bedazzled fawn, fight
To hug their trail deep in my skies.

I sit around on any day
Raving over the thoughts you bring.
It's always the most pleasant thing,
When your spirit deigns come my way.

The love of you gives no warning.
It tramples any happening
With thoughts one just would not think of.
It reigns over body and soul
And naturally has all control
And all matters, suddenly shoves.

The love of you, if I resist,
Resorts to get me off my piste.
So there I stand or rather hang,
Trying then to desparately fake
A facade my mind did not stake,
Like in an internal harangue.

The love of you is God given,
All my wants it comes to even.
It soothes aches, fills up misses,
Always fostering pleasant dreams
That stand loudly in smothered screams,
Revealing spiritual kisses.

It has the span of a lifetime.
It brands what it sees as its prime,
Gently rockabies the spirit,
Where it lives on, as its best treat.

The love of you knows no season,
It performs way beyond reason,
The living heart enlivening,
Giving it strength for one more beat,
The beats that arise as sees fit
The Maker of all living things.

The love of you seems to obsess
But rather it performs to bless
My soul from within which it basks.
At any given time it calms,
And to my desires gives alms
As I tread among daily tasks.

The love of you takes me to shores
Of isles I never knew before.
It makes me glide upon the wings
Of fierce eagles. Over wind blasts
They soar above what overcasts
The sun and its natural bling.

Through ups and downs and come what may
It thrives like buds in month of May
Though in the ears of the many
It sounds like a fake symphony.

The love of you is my banner
That I wave in bravely manner
Each time I face the wicked foe,
The one tripping my every stride
On this journey where we all ride
On whatever mean we may know.

The love of you sheds joyful tears
For through it all it has no fear.
It has lasted its span of time
And stands assured that its future,
Based on its past, is well secured
By the Word of the great I AM.

But since I know you love me too
For God always makes dreams come true
For the ones who crosses carry,
I daily give thanks and praises.
The few that this love amazes
Will be baffled when we marry.

The Lord backs up His promises
With subtle hints no one else sees.
Foolish would we be if ever
We'd go gamble our forever.

Your Face

I often consider from the depths of my heart
The reasons why I melt, losing all assurance,
Find it hard to focus, like having an infarct,
Fighting for every word, almost like in a transe.
Yet this inner snafu, this internal chaos,
Causing my heart to gear racing some Daytona,
Provokes in my psyche a strong surge of pathos.
Leaving me weak, fainty, just like a madonna.
This mother of feelings of my heart grabs a hold
And the knots I swallow seem to have many peers
And the smile I expose seems to favor pure gold
For it comes underline my many inner fears.
And I feel I should kneel, I'd be so much closer
To the ground that I feel I could hit anytime.
Since it is a posture adequate for prayer,
I pray hoping my voice rings not like a fake chime.
Painfully I attempt to show some composure.
I could always excell at keeping it inside,
And slowly deliver, carefully, with measure
This gush of affection, the love I cannot hide.
But deep within my eyes I know it can be seen
My lovely, jolly cause of instability.
Come and look into them and enjoy the whole scene,
Your pretty face my dear, of fair serenity.

Life Goes On

We toddle down the streets of life
Then comes the time when we mature
And deal with all that live's so rife
Till we're crushed by Mother Nature,
And as we feel her every prong
We try to mind the right and wrong
For no matter what life goes on.

The years follow like the seasons,
Nothing lasts long under the sun.
Nature puts a show all day long
But the night seems to offer none.
But in this Earth's merry-go-round
Where joys and miseries abound
At every sunrise life goes on.

Each one has an el dorado
That daily he attempts to reach
And through all acts of bavado
Battles till he gets to its niche.
As he grasps it, as it all seems
They come wake him up from his dream,
But he resets, and life goes on.

The most valued of all the days
Are the ones when love comes to town.
It comes rearrange all our ways
Then leaves us a pitiful frown
For as it stands nothing does last
Though some of us clench to the past
But still placidly life goes on.

And friends will come, and friends will go
In equal sharing as we hope,
But later we hear their echo
As we slowly go down the slope,
But the solace they often bring
Offsets the dread of their cold sting
But yet stoically life goes on.

Through fears and hope we live this life
Though we hope to hope more than fear
For steadily at every strife
The Spirit in us helps us steer.
To all needs the Father attends,
Dull is he who this truth, contends
For from the Spirit life goes on.

And sudenly we cease to walk
The surface of this God's green Earth.
We get invited to go stalk
Greater things on God's divine turf.
As this earthly life is no more
Spirit and soul to Heaven soar,
There truly, freely, life goes on.

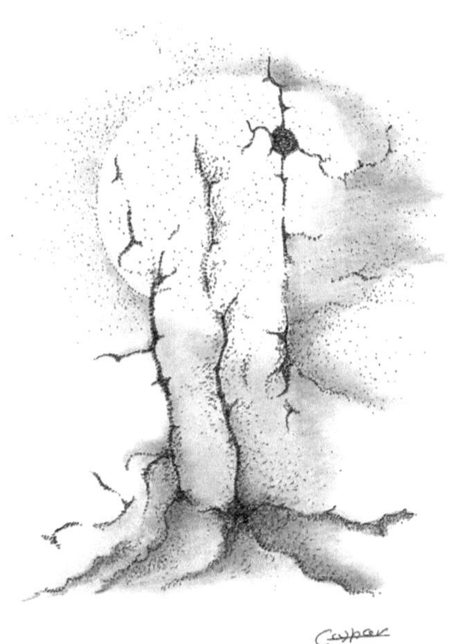

What If The Mother Was The Door

From the dawning shades of all times,
When there was but the Great I AM,
Your blessed name, bright and lowly,
Shone like the sun over the earth
For the Fruit of your precious girth,
God's handmade, O Virgin Mary!

Conceived to offset the downfall,
Willingly you answered the call
That resonated deep in you.
You were tailor made, the purest
And grace on you shine at its best,
Mother of a race made brand new.

You were thought of and realized
Even before Eve was chastised
For God sees time in all its scope.
But the first couple had its trial
But failed, causing the big downfall
That set the stage for mending hope.

So when God's plan fully matured
You shone in your perfect nature
And played your part most lovingly.
You opened up the earthly door
And like it's never done before,
The Creator trod earth humbly.

He came with love to redirect
His creatures lost, week and abject,
Kept in slavery under sin yoke.
They had managed by their doings
To upset the Supreme Being;
Spirits panting under flesh cloak.

So you receive the Spirit's Seed
Sent up this crumbling world to feed,
Light to shine through the earth darkness.
Beacon to lead on this journey
Done by the brethren, the many,
Created by God sheer goodness.

So He came in a poor manger,
Cold, dark like a common stranger,
The perfect Lamb of sacrifice.
Meek, humble although Almighty,
Obeying those whom He pities,
For thirty years honing the prize.

Often when lost in confusion
We should observe the foe's actions
For they lead to the most precious.
When the dark angel split the church,
Well aware of her divine touch,
He removed her most glorious.

For she's the mother most holy,
The precious gift from Calvary,
Bequeathed by the Font of wisdom,
Who knowing well her depths of heart,
Before He did from us depart
Put His brethren in her bosom.

After He paid for our freedom
By being most worthy ransom
He gave forgiveness and mercy.
And despite all the prongs and thorns
Still full of love yet so much scorned
He poured on us His clemency

For the Virgin did not need us,
She could have been assumed for thus
Was her role on this earth all done.
Just like Her Son through suffering
She had, through life of sword piercing,
Co-redeemed her race of its wrongs.

She had her Son but was assured
How much suffering she would endure,
Always humbly meditating
On what for Him life had in store
And silently the Mother bore
This dim future though God trusting

Yet through her life's daily toiling
She never ceased her pondering
Over what tomorrow will bear.
She is Mother to her lone Son
With love stirring like you've seen none,
Who'd quickly die His life to spare.

But no one will ever fathom
If I write now till kingdom come
The depths of love they had for realm,
They need not to communicate,
Through glance they could all modulate.
Their hearts the same prongs overwhelm'.

She was there in most everything,
When her sweet glance could solace bring,
Prompted His start, stood by His end.
When He completed His great task,
When was done what His Father asked,
She received her Lamb in her hands.

From any son you can gather
That when suffering, they'd rather
Not have their mother as witness.
Nothing to them is more painful
Than mother's face all sorrowful,
Enduring sword-piercing distress.

Her heart was pierced beyond compare,
Yet she stood there with loving stare,
Offering Her love on God's Throne
For the rabid stain of our fall,
For ransom demanded her All,
For there He hung, her flesh and bone.

See, the Spirit overshadowed
And the Word was flesh here below
But no gonad set was produced.
The Flesh and Blood that were slaughtered
Came from one source sin-unbothered.
The pure Virgin divinely spruced.

Nobody will ever fathom
The bond divine, beyond awesome
Between the Mother and the Son
And it's fitted that as a Queen
She oversees all divine scenes
As ladies of the house have done.

Yes Peter was given the key,
What he decrees, Heaven agrees.
The Lord set it this way afore.
But in His Mother's love, rightly
Who co-redeemed all so humbly,
He made her of Heaven the door.

And the poet prayed...

Serene and placidly, spreading over the vale
The night smothers the day and the owl shouts the tale.
A light breeze gently rocks baby birds on their hays,
The flowers seem to miss the caress of sunrays.
The lonely mocking bird, unfaithful in its ways
Seems to want to repent for its so many preys.
Even the air you breathe seems dainty to inhale
For placid and serene night falls over the vale.

I cherish these moments of calm and peaceful rest
When everyday voices from within weary chest
Decrease in decibels to die down in silence...
There my soul opens up, recalls its provenance.
At these painful hours summing all miseries,
When the world introspects arousing all queries
And the joys of the day have magically faded,
Simply I relinquish to these hours shaded
Peacefully invading the muffled surroundings
There Your Love permeates the core of every being,
Revealing Your goodness when the day expires.
Just like in Your heaven You ignite Your fires,
Enkindle in the hearts, O my Lord, Your Spirit...

On my knees I implore Your loving clemency
For the so many hearts ignoring Your Mercy.
Caught in the carnal world of making a living
You, the Source of all lives, they go daily missing.
I beseech You, my Lord, for the ones who feel shame
When the world proudly japes for they call on Your Name.
Lord, You always raise up the meek and the lowly
While for fleeting power this here world raves only.
To love and to serve You seem a waste of one's time,
So great many of us ignore the divine chime
Reminding the creatures to heed the Creator.

I beg for Your Mercy, O most loving Savior,
For the brokenhearted, for the withering soul,
In Your loving kindness, have pity, make them whole.
For the wandering kind, the ones who lost all hope,
Who became hard and cold, those who no longer mope.

Lord I also offer the narcissistic one
Who linger in the mire of loving self alone,
Caught in the dreary links of egotistic net
While loving his neighbor would change the world facet.
O Lord I pray also for the cold murderer
Who often repudiates the baptismal marker
That you give Your children as spiritual sticker.

For the sign of these times is that at early age
The sparrow of candor flees from the young child's cage,
And divine innocence, the key to happiness,
Cannot release the flow of the graces that bless
The heart who lovingly upholds all of Your laws.
So they go on marching, claiming rights for their flaws,
Drearily they become true spiritual outlaws.

O Master, remind them of Your plan the detail,
That Love alone matters and will always prevail,
For the least of the deeds done unto Your brethren
Your justice will always come make matters even.

The great spin

Under the glare of the hot sun
Where life thrives down to the unknown,
Under the mantle of the sun
We all strive with tasks of our own.

The birds pick at all they can find
The flowers suck up from the soil
The beasts to beasts are not so kind,
They battle hard to get their spoil.

But Mother Earth rolls rapidly
Half of hers chores, half of hers rests.
Always with care she steadily
Night and day serves her very best.

And we all go rollercoasting
We all enjoy her subtle ride
We all night and day do our thing
Caring for the ones by our sides.

For minding the brethren's always
The most important way to go.
It sets us up upon our ways
With blessings trickling down in row.

So there in the cosmos she springs
Rotating fiercely on axis
She has many children to bring
To light and warmth that they so miss.

Relentlessly she thrusts her mass
Around this so dangerous sun
Aware of what would come to pass
At the least misstep on her run.

So she goes day and she goes night
Keeping a keen eye on the glare
That at the same time, scorching might
Can nurture and give so much care.

Folks flout the impending danger
But yet she minds their well-being.
To her prowess they're all strangers,
Taking for granted her fleeing.

She brings her seasons and her rain
Her dear multitude to amuse
And steadily sings her refrain
To all the ones she keeps enthused

She crosses epochs and eras
Never missing a rendez-vous
Carrying so many auras,
The bright ones and dark ones she coos.

In her journey throughout the years
She's never missed on her mission
To show the God who gently steers
And keeps her in track and action.

For daily she reveals His love,
Her steadiness, His faithfulness.
His divine care comes from above
That with eyes shut one can witness.

She spins rapidly like a top
Yet never misses a sunshine
At light speed through each year, no flop,
Every season she brings is fine.

She swings oceans, she swings mountains
Yet her vales are not overflown.
The sea its bed of stone retains
And the mounts they stand on their own.

She cools herself and chosen crowd
By drawing water from the sea,
By forming huge and heavy clouds
That pour deluge when fit they see.

And she feeds, craddles and nurtures
Providing for all she carries.
She has all grains in her nature
And her harvest never tarries.

The richness deep in her bosom
Could feed the multitude she reels
As mother she wants them to come
And share with all rather than steal.

And so she goes by day by night,
Offering chores and giving rest
But rest assured, she has the might
Given to her to do her best.

The glow of her sister planet
Always caresses her dark side.
She spins like a lucent hornet
But next to Earth always abides.

They run and spin and do their thing
Always aligned not to bother
Steadily they follow their swing
While never nearing the other.

And yes she has other siblings
The clear firmament shows their shape
Some much bigger, others have rings
But none has the moon at its nape.

But she keeps her trajectory
Well secured by her Creator
No other star has history
As enticing to narrators.

Though at every spin of her run
Earth remains torn from pole to pole
Her beauty the galaxy stuns
Her archangels have firm control.

Under the warmth of the bright sun
That shines for one and shines for all,
Always when Earth by God is spun
His blessings over us befall.

Day And Night

Do you know why I love to hold you tenderly,
Why I can spend all time loving you faithfully,
It's because of my life, day and night, you only
Remain the lovely star leading me steadily.

The magic of your smile, your kind and lovely eyes,
The softness of your touch make you my dearest prize.
So day and night I long for that lovely surprise
That blessed day that will our love materialize.

This is the sole resaon in my heart from now on
Like a queen on her throne you will reign thereupon..
Be kind to your subject, ignore him not for long
You will make his delight day and night and thereon.

God's Love

Funny how it feels so strong
What we thought did not belong
Tween the both of us.

You remain the pinnacle
I thought could never tackle
Even if I'd burst.

But the love planted in us
Is an all miraculous
Gift from God above.

He created you and me
So that through monogamy
We may feel His Love.

The Mother

And she wakes up, her night half spent,
She's up early, her dreams all bent.
She looks kindly at her offspring
The two sunshines of her dull world
The apples of her eyes, her pearls
Those causing her heart chords to ring.

She ponders over tomorrow
Bringer of fears and of sorrow.
Having herself so much endured.
How much would she give of her life
For theirs not to be so pain rife
And she prays for their bright future.

For she had gone through misery
Suffered from farthest memory
But knows so well that through it all
Though all seemed bleak, bereft of hope
The means given for her to cope
Always came from the Lord of all.

He the Master, the Creator
He from whom trickles all splendor
Lovingly carries His children
From generations since of old
Through thick or thin, through heat or cold
Never faulting their daily grain.

Therefore she prays, Her best asset.
Their lives into His hands she sets.
And as she prays so fervently
As she surrenders at His feet
All her suff'rings and their merits
Pour blessings on her family.

Your Eyes

Lakes of the bluest waves
Reflect the sky above
And the clouds come and pave
A steady trail of love
Before never heard of.

And the sunny meadows
Bearing the month of May
Seem to give the rainbow
A colorful dismay
Worthy of pure Almay.

But when I see your eyes
At each glorious dawn
My soul all mesmerized
As ingenuous a fawn
Caught in the fairest lawn

Come whisper to my heart
Still in lunar slumber
Then the stampede that starts,
Sets fires bright amber
On walls of my chamber.

Your eyes, in the exile
Land where I don't reside
Set the mood on the isles
To rekindle the tide
Where my destiny hides.

Your eyes take for a spin
My soul and make it grow
Come the thick or the thin
Into a lovely glow
Of Winter's purest snow.

Ominous threat

There in the sky of somber coat
There all over, there, everywhere,
Birds are flying fast to denote
To us below, those who still care,
The reasons of this knot in throats.

But we all guessed what it could be,
We all pondered on its nature,
We all, old timers and newbies,
Wondered this time how to secure
This treasured land of Jollibee.

The moon in the sky gave its signs,
Its pallor everyone noticed.
Its soft light seems to trigger sighs
From the chests of those watching this
Impending ruin from these dark skies.

And on the lake where all swans rule,
Where the moon mirrors its kindness,
The birds seen usually so cool,
Just can't contain their nervousness.
Their instinct just cannot be fooled.

And so nightfall besets the land
Where the heartbeats are all racing.
Deep in the chests where all lives blend,
The lamps reveal in their shining
An atmosphere of pure doomland.

Night of terror, night full of dread,
Night meant for lovers to cuddle
But that now pitilessly spreads
On every lake, pond and puddle
This sense of fear, heavy as lead.

But tell me birds, you high above
You that perch high above the soil,
You the wild ducks or you the doves,
Whose business this ordeal comes spoil,
This trickles from what side of love?

O firmament that temper throws,
O firmament of blessings rife,
O firmament that all hearts knows
And keeps them pumping of your life,
Save us from these internal throes.

But here on Earth where simmer dreams,
Where all try to make them come true,
Where we don't even bother trim
The lies from the truth that is due,
We suffer from all that it seems.

Dreams on the mind, dreams in the heart,
Dreams that lessen daily hardship,
Dreams that gladden us from the start
And keep us from counting the sheep,
Come dry all tears that you impart.

As the Earth swaps its yin for yang,
As the sun blesses other shores,
As the shadows throw silent bangs
While all minds dream and deep throats snore,
Its other side deals with its pangs.

For the darkness only covers
Humanity's crucifixion.
For all sins silently hover.
In the spiritual addition
Nothing that's due is left over.

But the spirit all causes plead
For it sees what we'll never know
With silent tears, it stands livid
For its warnings loudly echoed,
When facing karma and its speed.

But the loud soundless threat remains
In the dark sky of everyone.
For some their sun never regains
Its shine by strong shadows outdone
And made eternal all their pain.

And all the firmament brightness,
All of the sacrements power,
All the sermons and their prowess
Their dark soul will never shower.
They cling hard to their hopelessness.

Right there above in their dark sky
With nightmares and loud snore in throats
Birds of all sizes are flying high,
To give account on bleeding notes
Of weaknesses the world swears by.

My Lord

From the depths of my soul I come to thy presence
With the wheels of my mind deflated, no essence
In what I want to be to run the few errands
My conscience wide awake received right from thy Hands.

But in my frightened heart, the pump where my life flows,
I have thy Word engraved, I uphold all thy laws.
Every beat of this heart says of thy Mightiness
And every breath I take thy Name, my Lord I bless.

Good Old July

In this my land of broken dreams,
Where all come apart at the seams,
All out of sync, before their time,
Like children when they lost their rhyme.

Like gliding winds on frozen lakes,
Forgotten thoughts of what's at stake,
The silent casts off a sorrow
That deep in your sand you burrow.

Through thick or thin the sun will shine
As a promise of love divine.
When it delivers your blessings
At your front door is where it rings.

And always when the sky is blue
Through the trees the sun winks at you.
Over nature shades of gladness
Bring about joy in every chest.

And all alone the paths one takes
Weeds and daffodils the sun bakes
Evenly all through the hot day
Until the rain, the sky comes spray.

They bring songs to Mother Nature
All caught in daze of her rapture.
She takes all in and so shivers
In turn fragrances delivers.

Every atom of air exults
Praising God in silent tumult.
The tree with wooden poker face
All evenly receive the grace.

And so July always simmers,
Claiming the essence of summer
And though nature's in a hurry
She never misses January.

The waves repossess all the dunes
Crafted during the month of June.
They come caress, ever daring,
The shore and all its living things.

And the sea roars, fierce and mighty
Crowning each wave with foam salty,
Steadily flowing broken dreams
Come to remind of this life stream.

This state of things is so fragile
Yet glides on shore of every isle
To bring right out of every soul
The love that deep inside it holds.

Then spurs right out of every chest
A hymn or tune bound to attest
That deep within, where life lingers,
Hope evermore remains stronger.

Hand in hand, well aware or not,
The mirrors of all broken thoughts
Reflect the rebirth of the hopes
Reminding not to brood and mope.

For all is forever given,
Falling on the laps now and then,
Rolling freely from Heaven's slopes
Solely with prayer as a dope.

It's related among seasons.
The skeptic ignores the reasons
But when at his front door it knocks
He only sees a stroke of luck.

Deep inside amid of all this
I feel overcome by the bliss.
All somber thoughts washed by the sea
And I fall at the wave mercy.

I long forgot the time of day.
And whereabouts of month of May
Lay much too heavy on my mind;
So much I left the world behind.

Always, always with no warning
Your cello can play lighter strings
For under heaven's canopy
You see how stars can be floppy.

But all the while as the sun bakes,
Fixing Mother Nature's mistakes
The raging waves come and attune
All life aspects on every dune.

And so nature will never fail
Regardless of what it entails,
To bring about in due season
Blessings for all hidden reasons.

Mirage

Conversing on the phone, fell in love with the voice,
Hoping it'd be surging from an adequate source.
I could not help myself, did not have any choice
Admiring this face, my heart increased in force.

Ravishing, beautiful, exquisitely jovial,
Over the ones I've known,, you reign as prettiest.
Sincerely I love you, please won't you be my pal?
Silently I will wait, my poor heart will not rest.

Blesséd Hope

If I still write these lines, O my dear one, they're all for you
So you'll come to me and kindle this old flame anew.
If I still jot verses, my loved one, they'll speak of you,
You the soul I seek and will pursue my whole life through.

I keep deep within every single of these instants
When breathing the same air, we could shut the door to the world,
Feeling so complete for to each other so present,
Nothing we thought could come and take away our precious pearl.
There was no need for words, the exchanged glances knew so well,
Funny how love could flow straight from Heaven's blessed well.
But deep inside me stirs the hopes that my love, swell.

If I write these poems, my darling, they all speak of you,
Of you the angel I dedicate my whole life to
If I scribble again silently I plead with you
That one day you'll return and be my mistress anew.

So many attempts I made to chase you off my mind,
Painted you with darkness, when the heartaches would overwhelm,
When the air was lacking, from my missing you too blind,
When no one would compare, of my heart you had the helm.
I'd jump at the call of your name, sweetest sound to hear,
Would follow strangers, when I think you are near.
But I keep faithfully the hope that dries my tears.

If I write these stanzas where your name rings through and through
It's just to remind you that my love for you is true.
If I write these quatrains where I seem to beg of you
It's so you come back and be my loving squeeze anew.

Don't shed the tears

Don't shed the tears, my heart,
Come out of your alcove,
Don't shed the tears, my heart,
Don't be afraid to love.
Her heart may be fickle,
Drift away a little,
Let it be, let it go.

Don't shed the tears, my heart,
Regain your composure.
Don't shed the tears, my heart,
Beat at the same measure.
Time always comes to heal
The worst pain you might feel
And frees us from sorrow.

Don't shed the tears, my heart,
Come, come and dry your tears.
Don't shed the tears, my heart
Bring to the Lord your fears.
In many ways before
For love of you He bore
Your burdens long ago.

Town Quiesence

Over the garden in the street
Catch the echo steady racket,
Either toiling, loud epithets,
Life goes on while laundry is neet

Hanging under a rusty sun,
Amid the evening aromas,
Stiffling the day and its dramas,
As a tocsin's rung by some nun.

A grinder cart timbres away,
Drowning in the day steady fuss
The soft horn of a public bus
Emerges then it treads its way.

And as the dusk colors the day,
A cloud unveils a moon quarter,
Nature again sees the barter,
The night the day upstage away.

Don't make a sound, feel the silence
Always so fleeting, so subtle,
Come closer and in love cuddle,
In this town and its quiescence.

Turgeau

Faces of the late seventies,
Anchored deep in my memory,
I see your trace in a hurry
As my younger brother I tease.

Loudly the sun glides on the porch,
The shoe shiner his change awaits.
The fowl declines the rooster date
So distasteful was its approach.

And soon the old maid will depart
Well imbued of her instructions.
The different kind of provisions
Will have to fit in her old cart.

The first meal that she has prepared
Seems to have pleased every palate.
The stomach of the whole estate
For which so many years she cared.

Loudly now resonates the horn
Of this bright decorated van.
It comes always this time past ten
With those so many flags adorn'.

The four corners of that old house
Have come alive to say the least.
That young made frantically assists,
Before he boards, this youngster's blouse.

Then my mother to us reminds
That time awaits no one ever,
That minding it is thus clever
Or else this puts you in a bind.

After a long trepidant rush
The bunch will get ready to leave
For school, not before they receive
From the Spirit the silent touch.

I push open the old green gate
And shuffle lively through the crowd.
The lines of cars with horns out loud,
To move ahead are desperate.

The crowd of kids lugging book bags
Thickens with each passing minute
And forcing through your way in it
Demands skills and a vernal drag.

And the cars sing and this echo
Into the ears makes a carnage
And the large crowd holds you hostage
While waving in the Canado.

Petty merchants are all around
Offering their variety.
Cigarettes, cookies and candies,
Any kind of snack can be found.

But lo! There, crossing the corner
With the cop directing the peak
Of this all bottleneck traffic
With flow that'd slow any "flanneu".

Now turn into the gas station
With two overwhelmed attendants,
Ignoring how it's not prudent
To smoke during their transactions.

And the kids sitting in the cars,
For the most part still half asleep
Frantically taking a last peep
At some reading undone thus far.

While in the blue car up ahead
The voice of an irate mother
Seems to the kids bring no bother
For they too have eyelids of lead.

And you walk down this busy street
Through the small crowd of the Kinder
That today seems to be kinder,
All kids are brought into their seats.

All of a sudden emerges
That noise crowning above the crowd.
It resonates, drilling so loud
Then it dies down and resurges.

This old house with the iron gate
Where that old dog chased me one day,
On the front porch where it once lay,
Offers no clue of the pooch fate.

See this great wall Evangelist
Announces the parochial school
Whose yard offers a khaki pool
Of kids in row to say the least.

And still the parents in hurry
Come disembark their progeny.
Softly you hear Serge Regiani
Amid the morn silent fury.

Everyone rush to be somewhere.
Life is brewing, percolating
And this episode recurring
Brings no change to this thoroughfare.

Drivers are vociferating
Enraged at this slow-moving string
Of cars tangled up in this sting
Of two guys street excavating.

Now this explains that noise once heard
That was so loud but yet unseen.
This is the reason why obscene
Exchanges fly amid this herd.

From afar you hear church bells ring.
It's eight o'clock in this quarter
But Au Galop did not falter
To gather in the folks' offspring.

Then as usual I leave Turgeau
And veer into CRA road.
A truck full of gravel downloads
The street to repair undergo.

Hence was of my old neck of hood
A glimpse of morning rush hour,
And such memories still devour
My heart as often as they would

For there were rooted all my hopes
And there as well sprang my crosses
That life mercilessly tosses,
Of its journey you can't elope.

Every fiber of my being,
Every stroke of acquired strength
Mastered subtly but at great length
Was hewn from this era I sing.

All Yours

Gotta tell you, buddy of mine,
What I hope will make you happy.
I tried hard not to be so kind
But this rests heavy on my mind
So I'll hand it to you, poppy.

This lady for which we both drool,
The one with the riveting smile,
Put us in a spot not so cool,
An entanglement made for fools
That's been hurting us for a while.

Many times we almost engaged
In more than a verbal debate,
With justified yet silent rage.
But unwilling to turn the page
We sadly suffer the same fate.

I tried from her to get away.
Hoping some sweet day to regroup
And gladly love again someday.
In safer arms, see come what may,
Unwilling to stay where we stoop.

But now to you I leave it all.
Take her away to your Eden.
For me her world is much too small.
No two stallions can fit this stall,
Take her away into your den.

I gave her all the love I could.
I gave while she did the taking.
I closed my eyes more than I should
And justified her attitude
To soothe my heart she was breaking.

On this spinning globe what you throw
Never fails to splash in your face.
It comes always to you although
You can fly high or go hide low.
It always, always finds your trace.

If one day under your sweet love,
She groans out someone else's name,
Some name so far never heard of,
Since you will be couple betroth'
Silently gives yourself the blame.

Have I

Have I known you before
To feel for you this way?
Have I known you before,
Before you came my way?
It seems that from the start
In the realm of my heart
Your name was all over.

Have I loved you before
To yearn for you this way?
Have I loved you before
Before my night was day?
For it feels that with you,
Completed and brand new,
I am born all over.

My living has no sense
If my life you don't fill,
It was not worth a pence
Till you came and you kill'
That ever growing pain
Of dreadful loneliness
That would always remain
Were not your gentleness.

Have I loved you before
To long for you this way?
You, the one I adore,
Who take my breath away.
For when I hold you near
Gazing into your eyes,
Slowly I see my sphere
Take form, materialize.

Desamor

When I sit and take it all in
I feel so lost while traveling
The labyrinth of all your lies,
The very cause of all my sighs

I went bright eyed and bushy tailed
On your vast sea without a sail
Putting all trust in your brown eyes,
Surfing your waves of any size.

I had put all my trust in you,
In your sea and your sky so blue,
But I was riding a mirage,
So well hidden by your visage.

Now dejected down to the soul,
Traumatized by all I was told
I shun now every talk of love
Keeping my heart in its alcove.

No love vows as they all promise,
No sweet nothings, no talks of bliss,
Whether as a joke or for real
They disrupt my peace of heart still.

For me all was so true and bright,
All my wrongs you came and made right,
So naturally rolled down my lips
Rose tenderness, warmth of tulips.

But no longer will I utter
Any sweet word in cheap chatter.
I will no longer trust in them
Since my heartache they cause to stem.

The sucker punch my heart endured
Taught me a lesson, this I'm sure.
Twas a steep price, I won't forget,
And don't perceive any reset.

So don't talk to me about love
No one will come my heart to shove.
I took it hard but grasp it well,
No one to me cheap lies will tell.

The road is long, of souls so full,
But dark ones have the sweetest pull,
They take pleasure at your demise
To them you're just a common prize.

Mighty deeds

And for a long, long time
We waited for this time.
Time of peace, time of joy,
Free of the least alloy.
Time that will make us see
That among the many
Who came seeking a break,
We too had what it takes
To make it yet so far,
While many lost their star.

For long, long time ago,
Searching high, searching low,
We always came up short
Of peace of any sort.
So we went on faking
To every human being
While what we had inside
Was nothing else but pride
And the sole reason why
Peace to us was so shy.

But now we understand,
It's been so well explained,
That what you so receive
And that so often grieves
Is drawn from the many
Acts that first we carry.
So always keep in mind
That you ought to be kind
For your deeds have power
To bring tears or laughter.

Honor, Praises and Glory

To the greatest act of Love
Christians come on bended knee,
Join your tears to the tale of
His sufferings for the so many.
Since it is for our offenses
That the Lord suffers today,
Melted by His sufferances
Live and die following His way.

Kneeling in the garden alone
Deep within He suffers the strife,
HE fears, hopes and prays His prone,
Begging: "Father, please spare my life!"
At times the fear envelops Him,
At time love seems the only choice,
But finally love's divine scheme
Rings aloud with a stronger voice.

Judas possessed, in his wile,
Accosts Him, with infamy.
He kisses Him … and meanwhile
Hands Him to His enemies!
Judas, we get on your trail
Every time we, by our sins,
The beloved Lord we fail
Causing over His sufferings.

HE's abandoned at the mercy
Of a horde of raging demons,
And over His face you can see
The traces of their weapons.
You should have, O angels faithful,
Witnessing their wrongdoing,
Spare Him from this act most awful
Or destroy this throng of fiends.

They dragged Him to the high priest
Who backs up their vile doing,
And raising his cursed fist
Accuses Him of blaspheming.
When He 'll come to judge the world,
This Savior and His justice,
When His thunder will unfurl,
He will accuse you of all this.

As He goes through His ordeal
All conspire to torment Him.
Even Peter losing his zeal
Denied being part of His team
But Jesus pierces his soul
With the most tender of glance,
Since to him this was foretold,
Bitter regrets make him wince.

Before Pilate they compare Him
To a louse though He never was.
Oh! But what a most vile scheme
To Him they choose Barabbas!
But what a dreadful sight to see,
The righteous one's forsaken,
They condemn Him with no mercy
But the crime is forgiven.

So they strip Him and they bind Him,
At Him each throws his anger.
And this spotless Lamb now seems
To withstand their blows no longer.
We are all the real victims,
Desist O cruel tormentors!
Come and pour your hatred steam
On us the true perpetrators.

And a wretched crown of thorns
Pierces His most divine head.
To Him archangels adorn,
Worldly thugs, you taunt with stead.
And He languishes in pain,
And suffers down to His soul
While you delight as you spend
On you glories you extol.

He walks and He climbs Calvary
Laden by this weighty wood.
From there like on pulpit, carries
His voice as loud as He could,
"Father, spare them, I beg of you,
For they know not what they do."
That's for Christians a way brand new
To revenge when they're done unto.

A large mutinous troop shouts
And insulting Him as they scream:
"If of this bind He comes out,
Oh yes, we will believe in Him!"
Easily He can desist
The torture He undergoes
But He just cannot resist
This great Love His Heart echoes.

Ah! From Your throne of torture
Lord of lords, please do not descend.
By Your power, keep Your tenure,
Remain there until the end.
But please, keep Your solemn promise
And pull us all by Your grace,
So to obtain heavenly bliss
Keep us all right in Your trace.

He expires and all nature
In Him mourns the Creator.
On earth there is no one creature
That does not grieve for its Author.
Such a terrible spectacle
Would not it melt down my heart?
Unless I am hard to tackle
Like the hardest stone of art.

Souvenirs

Should always remember
Your days of love fever
For in life if ever
Your loved one moves farther,
Causing you to wither
You will have thereafter
Souvenirs to treasure.

My Soul

My soul do you savor
The all-divine caress
Of your loving Master?
Tell me, does He impress
Your inner most fiber?
So put on your best dress
He awaits your lover.
He did largely confess
For you His affection.
So don't settle for less
But this divine union.
He remains the fortress
And the best companion
Of your days in distress.

Love bliss

Never when love blesses our shore
Has it given any warning
It lands softly within the core
And it's so thrilling.

And right there we are dumbfounded,
Right there, hung snuggly by its hook,
Right there we're gently elated
By the ease it took.

My most beautiful love song
Is sung to the love of my life,
No matter the land she grew on
She'll come settle my every strife.

It rains down its golden droplets
On hearts that pine from fondness drought,
And right there give them clear outlets
To chase sullen pouts.

It comes clearer than any dawn
To change the landscape of the face,
With gentle rays it warms their lawns,
Blots the dark holes trace.

It redirects their every step
Away from hatred darkened halls
For it only hears sounds that leapt,
Bouncing off Heavens' blissful walls.

And we see tests, proofs and all toils
As means to render it stronger,
For it grows amid all turmoil
And lasts way longer.

It takes the souls that meet down here,
Predestined to receive its bliss,
To the heavens among their peer
Whose sufferings have ceased.

To me the sweetest love of all
Is the one who will come my way,
She already has heard my call,
And one day will land, come what may.

For years will come, and years will go,
Raining down all their miseries,
But in the heart all love will grow,
Brewing reveries,

Reflecting what is deep inside,
Reflecting what the mind is fed,
Reflecting what the Spirit hides,
All by Heavens led.

And so we go through life's journey
Carried in arms of the Father.
HE gives suckers to so many
Good and bad, till the great Gather.

One day happy, and one day sad,
On this well known rollercoaster
Of this the brain can become mad,
Reading its poster.

But all the while the bliss remains,
Enthralling the young and the old.
We love the joys, suffer the pains,
Making the heart bold.

But never would have we traded
This feel any other to spouse.
Love never leaves a soul jaded,
Ever ready its world to douse.

Adoration

Give praises to the Lord, all who on earth are living,
Come all on bended knee!
In the Host let's adore the God-man, our God-Kin
With fresh incense and sweet harmony. -- Refrain

With hymns of thanks giving and gladness
Let's praise the Lord and His Heart so clement
And for His kindness confess:
O Lord we adore You, in the Blessed Sacrament! (2)

Never fathomable is His ocean of mercy,
The Lord loves us so much!
On the altar displayed, He sheds all past secrecy
At His feast He wants us all to rush. -- Refrain

He dwells within us all, our Redeemer and Master,
So kind and so loving.
He remains forever the Victim and good Pastor,
He leads us always to His Dwelling. -- Refrain

In the manger, newborn, He comes to us as Brother,
His might and divinity shed.
On the cross, as ransom, He's the Lamb of the Father,
At the mass, He's the true living Bread. -- Refrain

To My Baby

What would we gain from it,
What would we benefit
From such moment as this,
That we'd seal with a kiss?
Will it make us complete?
Say, what we'd gain from it?

They pulled our hands apart
But we did not lose heart.
Though they thought it was wrong
We kept the loving strong.
Why can't we for our sake
His blesséd Word partake?

We swore on the first day
To follow in His way.
We should before we dine
Taste of His Bread and Wine
And secure in our chests
That Love with which He bless'.

What would we gain from it
But weaken our spirits?
For sure we'd touch the sky
But not His Heavens' high.
Will it make us complete
Or such blessing deplete?

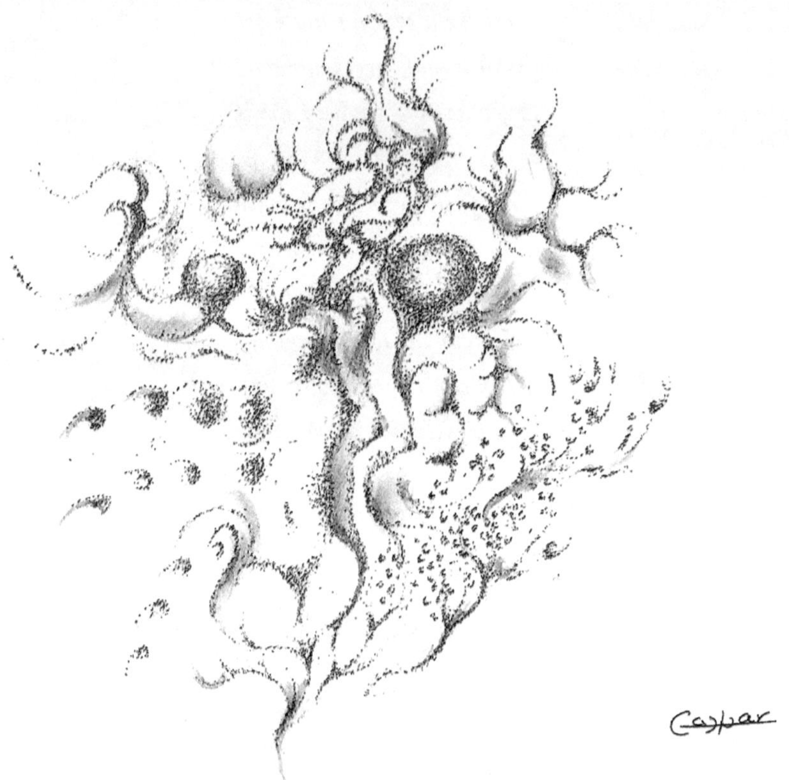

Caspar

Down the road

(Air of "As it was")

Deep in your eyes,
Right there so deep in your eyes,
I can see but coldness instead
But you want to cuddle in bed.

Standing confused,
Of kissing not at all enthused,
All you say I've already heard,
Your actions are drowning your words.

Ooooooh!
Here we stand, you and I,
You know we will make it down the road
Here we stand, please don't cry,
There's always someone else down the road,
Down the road
Down the road

Try to be strong
You know we'll have to go on
Many before us went that way
Really nothing left to be said.

Of all our plans
I can see that nothing remains.
It's always easy to break a heart,
Now just walk away with your part

Oooooh!
Here we stand, you and I,
You know well we'll make it down the road,
Here we stand, don't you cry
We will laugh of all this down the road,
Down the road
Down he road.

But no I won't tell,
I'll let them know you did well
They'll go all and crucify me,
Curse my assumed bigamy.

Ooooooohh! Here we stand!

First kiss

A rose blossomed upon your lip,
Early fruit of your virgin love.
I felt your tenderness so deep
That it carried me high above.

Sweet fragrance of innocent years,
Unending source of joy divine,
If my heart's still fighting its fears,
Remain the chill within my spine.

Only silence surrounded us
When to my love you gave your lip.
Oh! How I wish I could adjust
And not tremble when my heart flip'.

I delight in this first moment
When full of love and hearts ponding
We exchanged the kindred fragment
Of every ounce of that feeliing.

Sweet ray of your very first dawn,
Keep your very first kiss of love
Deep in your heart. So that upon
It shower blessings from above.

Love refrain

So jolly it sounds the refrain
Of this love that I sing to you.
So jolly and it's not in vain,
That I holler it through and through.

The birds in the air put a halt
To their daily frolicking chant,
The flowers silently exalt,
Their fragrances in the air spent.

The brook conveys to the willows
The cadence of its every score,
In return they bow very low,
Showing gladness right from the core.

Always with lyrical prowess
It sings of you, my sharona,
You my most blessed of mistress,
The precious part of my manna.

Of this love refrain I sing you,
The jolly air will always ring
For where there's love, there I'll see you,
Who to my heart happiness, bring.

Once we had

Once we had
Lots of years ahead of us,
Once we had
Teachings to make us pious,
Once we had
Will power to remain just,
Once we had
Drives galore to be unjust,
Once we had
Lots of time to readjust,
Once we had…
But failed many times and plus
Till we had
Within us the Lord Jesus.

The bed we no more share

This lonely bed ladden
Of treasured souvenirs
Upon which you lay then
When toward you I'd steer,
That yet keeps so concealed
The stormy escapades,
The times I'd make appeal
When you suffered mood trade,
Offers a silent stare,
This bed we no more share.

This relic that remains
Witness of our debates
That often put a strain
On our romantic state,
Remembers the long nights
You stayed awake wondering,
Concerned by all the fights
That our bond were tearing,
Keeps all with no fanfare
This bed we no more share.

In condolence with all my pain
Watches me reach for you in vain,
And of this love tearing me wide apart
Wonders will it one day from me depart?

This bed of me and you
That now misses you blind
That sends muttered boohoo
To strangers that it finds,
Trespassing on your turf,
This spot I hold so dear
And that it keeps reserved,
That's to my heart so near,
Feels like: how can I dare,
On it we no more share.

This oh so lonely bed
Will span through life right here,
This life heavy as lead
That your mere absence sears,
This bed would give its life
To wrap you in its sheets,
Satin caress' so rife
All to a queen so fit,
Hold you in loving snares,
This bed we no more share.

This wooden bed so strong
Soothes all my aches away,
Sorting where they belong
The weary thoughts I lay,
Faithfully, patiently,
Humble deep in the core,
It longs for silently
For you, dreams of encore,
This bed of solitaire
That now we no more share.

I always wonder

I always wonder what it would be
To be touched by an angel
To fly
To be free
To reach out the stars
To find a place
To look down and see
To be away from this cruel word
Letting out the girl I want to be.

I always wonder how would it feel
To come down on you
To travel deep within
To reach out your heart and find the key
To search for a safe place, my sadness
And sins to burry in.

I might not have the wings to fly
I might not have the key to your heart
But I still know how to reach the sky,
I know how to keep love from falling apart.

I give my soul
To the one my heart starts to beat
Because I believe in true love
And in candles which for ever stay lit.

Even when my world gives up on me
And everything looks like a dead end
I still get on my knees
And power to go on from God I lend.

And knowing that you are by my side,
It makes me believe
I am a sweet little angel
Sent from above with love to give.

Peace and Love

Peace on Earth, Peace to all men
Says to us the great "I AM"
Peace on Earth, Peace to all men
And resound the loud Amen.

This Peace the Lord gives to us,
Is fruit of divine Mercy
For indeed, the Lord Jesus
Gives so much for the journey.

This Peace therefore, as I say,
Is a precursor of Love.
It is always wished this way
So they mention Peace and Love.

Bathing in the Peace divine
Then our hearts open to Love.
On the face grace comes and shines
His Kingdom falls from above.

Peace again to men on Earth,
Peace the Lord bestows freely
And then Peace to Love gives birth
For us to see God's glory.

If One Day

If in your life one day
A good friend comes your way,
Remember He did say
He's here with us to stay.

If in your life one day
Your blue sky turns to gray,
Be strong, don't go astray,
Think of Heaven and pray.

If in your life one day
You meet her, don't delay.
Gives thanks to Him, I say.
I'm still alone today.

If in your life one day
Your soul He calls His way,
Trust in Him, He did say:
"I am Truth, Life and Way".

Star of life

I held so many hands, so many walked my way,
Kept many in my arms, others just ran away,
So many ones I begged, so many who forgot
Even my very name or the good side I got.

I made all promises that away have faded,
I had my share of flings that left me so jaded,
I believed in a few, was mislead by others,
While many to my croon would not even bother,

But all the while my dear, all those so many whiles,
I dreamt of you my love, of you my shiny star,
There was always something of you that, all beguiled,
Compelled me to press on but you remained afar.

There were times I regret and others I retained,
Quick instants of pleasure, and moments that now stain,
Times so clear I could swear that it was the right thing,
And the so many times of careful regrouping.

Now that gone are the days of hormonal parade,
Of mirage following and of clever charades,
I still deep in my mind entertain some prospects,
But in the midst of all, each time I introspect

It is you that I see my blessed guiding light,
You who gives to my life a clear trail to follow,
You who keep me going even in my dark night,
You I've been dreaming of, as I journey solo.

Before An Old Computer

Finally as it seems
In time before I scream,
I made it to the part
Where I can safely start.

I did not lose my hope,
Kept steadily the scope
Though in times it appears
I would pull off my ears.

So here I am, I said.
But why am I delayed?
No, I just discovered
I have nought to offer.

Fierceness

If you could see through me, my dear,
You'd jump so high, you'd brag so loud,
You'd stay awake at night from fear
Of losing me, feeling so proud.

If you could see through me, my love,
You'd pray all day, you'd pray all night,
Giving thanks to the God above
For a treasure of such a might.

I remain the captive that will never escape,
The one caught in you cage of bars of purest gold,
The one who willingly fix each and every gape,
The one who would not leave based on what was foretold.

If you could see through me, I say,
There would be stars in your blue sky,
There'd be warmth in your winter days,
And birds would sing when you'd go by.

If you could see through me you'd see
The fierceness of my love for you,
Strong enough to cross any sea,
Strong to make all your dreams come true.

Lustation

Whenever I'm given somebody nice and kind,
There is always a witch in the back of my mind.
There, in the dark alleys of my untamed desire
She paces restlessly and ignites my fire.

Seems though I'm not aiming at anyone's offense,
The grass is just greener the other side of fence.
And for every blessing the Lord on us bestows,
The devil always tries to spoil our tomorrow.

Someone like you

The first time I saw her face
I fell right into her trace.
It is not every Sunday
That suddenly comes your way
Someone like you.

She was jolly, and peppy,
Making her whole world happy,
On that lovely autumn day,
She went rolling on the hay,
As you would do.

So I asked her for her name,
What country she gives such fame,
She giggled then looked at me,
Weighing my anatomy
Like angels do.

For a while I felt impelled
Standing there under her spell,
To ask if she'd ever met
Anyone just like her set,
Someone like you.

Instead we chatted along,
Had to find ways to prolong
This encounter so bizarre,
Unprecedented thus far
With one like you.

I poured my heart easily,
Almost like making a plea.
She took all with empathy,
As though my life was worthy
Of one like you.

Of herself revealed nothing,
As if she had no meaning,
Willfully took the back seat
Just like had done in repeat
Someone like you

Then she explained earnestly
Like a muttered homily
That patience was a virtue
Regarded in highest view
By those like you,

That I should never desist
Keeping my mind on the piste
Of my heart where God reveals
The goodness that us here, fills,
All our lives through.

For often my hope wavers,
Its light gets feeble, quivers,
And I slip in some despair,
Aiming at other affair,
That wouldn't be you,

Human beset with weakness,
We often shape our own mess,
Trusting in any mirage
Bound to be some cheap potage,
Not one like you.

So we devise some quick plan
That we know well will not stand,
But the surging of the drive
Incites our miserable live
To then miss you.

All over were autumn leaves,
Tossed around as nature breathed.
They brought about steadily
Caresses unevenly,
Right 'pon us two.

The breeze blew a bit nippy,
But this floral entropy
Marveled my indigent soul,
Of my words I took control,
Still naming you.

And she did what she does best,
Remained silent for the rest,
As wanting to hear it all,
As sparing me from this fall
Deep into you.

Twice I offered her my coat,
Twice she rejected the quote.
She seemed to enjoy the breeze
That now was rocking the trees,
So unlike you.

Twas a Thursday, I recall,
One most precious day of fall,
And the air with drops of dew
Tickles with a scent brand new
All the way through.

The lawn under its blanket
Missed the sun that came to set,
Therefore the lake took it all,
Got gilded by nature call,
Blinding us two.

And the day ended softly
I had said all eagerly
Now the silence around us
Felt strange, made me curious.
I thought of you.

I took it she was thinking
Understood that was her thing
Not realizing that meanwhile
She let me stew in the pile
Said about you.

What she said to me after
Caused no sorrow nor laughter.
It came blunt but softly said
Over my mind made its raid,
Ceased thoughts of you.

There I remain all haggard
Because now she held the cards.
She had just kindly silenced
My mind of your love so tensed
By tales of you.

And so we walked hastily
This park was cold suddenly
To the street where leaves still flew
Carrying in sheer snafu
All that was you.

She had ransomed my psyche
Of this bind much to freaky
That lasted a small epoc
And left my heart in a shock
Pining for you.

Solitude

What do I say of solitude?
That she's the worst of companion,
That better is the multitude,
That it's like living in prison.

But I declare of solitude
That she begets the perfect art,
For the soul finds the fortitude
Once given to it from the start.

Frankly Speaking

I will never pursue, nor envy, nor covet
In any circomstance anyone else's pet.
The yearning of the flesh becomes a great offense
For anything greener on any side of fence.

So I'll remain faithful to my basic concept,
Not eager to create any spiritual debt.
If loving to the soul is the most soothing balm,
The craving for others' is the worst of napalm.

One day

One of these blessed day
I will say
Come what may
And fly to her embrace
To her place
See her face.
For so long I hunger
Holding her
Much closer
That in my dreams at night
I'd delight
At her sight.
So this day finally
In hurry
Not lonely,
I'll take her in my arms
Full of charm
To disarm
All the doubts in her mind
Set to bind
Us behind.
I'll say to her: "Baby"
"My chérie,
My Honey",
Gazing into her eyes
Lovely prize
And realize

That since eternity
I and she
One body
Were missing each other,
Much longer
Did suffer.
So from this moment on
Holding on
To her strong
We'll start our foyer
Happier
Forever.
The loveliest treasure
To ensure
Sheer pleasure
In the blessed action
Of union
And junction
That Heaven set apart
From the start
For the heart
For it last a lifetime
Making chime
Of love prime
Since they would realize
It's a prize
To be wise.

Beyond the clouds

With wings to fly, with open air,
With devotion and steady care,
A genuine love, like yours and mine,
Will make us ride upon cloud nine.

In the dawning of any day,
Far from the many come-what-may's
We will secure daily blessings
Straight from the Maker of all things.

All through the day we will exchange
Talks and concessions of all range.
Always giving to the other
The so sought-for place of honor.

And when the shadows of the night
Come and make all that's wrong look right,
With tender passion and much love
I'll show you what my heart's made of.

And when all drenched and all weary
I'll love you again, my chérie,
With devotion and steady care
And strong wings in the open air.

Happy Valentine

On Valentine the cards will pour
Because that's what the day is for.
But deep inside within my heart
I wish that we would never part.
Roses are for a protocol
Chocolate raises cholesterol,
But only God can make us feel
The love which our hearts does fill.
I love you, Happy Valentine
To a beautiful girl who's mine!

Pray

Pray my little child, pray. Pray when you're feeling down.
When from this life turmoil you can only get frown.
When the loving Savior your soul wants to restore
You have to willfully unveil it's every pore.

It is not made avail to every one of us
This sublime privilege, this sweet call of Jesus,
Inviting the sinner laden, down on his knees
From his flesh strong demands for everything it sees.

Your soul forever thirsts for His consolations,
And for His divine touch never has rejections.
It always comes begging, worn out and weakened
For the strength of His love, the power of His Hand.

After many a falls one day you'll realize
That your loving Master who often you despise,
Suffers from your contempt, and from your heart coldness.
He who waits peacefully to give you His richness.

He who made you at first model of His image
Will never let the world your spirit hold hostage.
You should therefore to Him, in sheer humility,
Dedicate all your life and pray for His mercy.

So pray my sweet child, pray, for the good Lord above,
He who created all just to show you His love,
Will give of this I'm sure, to you the very best.
Just put your trust in Him and let Him do the rest.

Flushing, 09/10/1997

When you love

When you love that someone
You can feel in a bliss,
Your world take teint and tone
Of her every caprice.

When you love that someone
You feel deep in your soul
That for so long alone
You're finally made whole.

For loving you so deep
Is to me the sweet task
The Lord wants me to keep,
That for so long I ask.

You are my light of day
Shine on my tarnish nights.
O darling come and stay,
Set my world ever bright.

For when you love someone
As much as I 'dore you,
You feel fit for a throne,
Your deepest wish come true.

And then there were none

How many a young men, how many young fathers
Who left ever eager to fight the enemy,
Lulled by selected words of skillful recruiters
To fall right in the midst of this world infamy.

They were trained for the most to face all kinds of war,
Were prepared to affront fiercest adversaries
But one important piece is still missing so far,
A motive that would come to quell their inquiries.

For what was the reason to shed so precious blood,
What would be the profit of such a sacrifice?
What would change the karma of this land that they trod,
Why despite history we fell in this trap twice?

So many mums and dads, so many wives and kids,
Left without their children or still missing their spouse.
Some with help of a friend, others, from fear, livid,
Alone wishing, praying that they're back to the house.

Just a few years ago they were playing the same
On a Nintendo screen, practicing day and night.
But now the threat is real, it's no longer a game,
They're killing human beings or they feeling the fright.

So far no end in sight, so far there's no way out.
The plans are washed out, no one saw this coming.
What was so cut and dry, so carefully laid out
Is now a sheer chaos with death daily roaming.

So many ways the world tried to prevent this hell,
So many times they were reminded not to go.
So many times because of news you cannot tell
The country silently suffered this heavy blow.

And the rest of the world, in favor or appalled,
Witness' the biggest mess known to this century.
And down in history it will be justly called
The start of the downfall of this blesséd country.

How many body bags, how many heads will roll
In this modern version of Apocalypto?
How many families will have to pay this toll?
On both sides of this war their painful tears echo.

Surely all our heroes daily stumble and fall
Under the grinding teeth of that beast to be fed
But woe to whoever would have started it all,
Better it would've been not to've been born instead.

For the shedding of blood of any God's creature
Under any banner that fits your agenda,
In return will demand the adequate measures
To clean the heavy stain painted on your aura.

I salute the many, for the most part unknown,
Forced into this carnage from fear of reprisal.
The ones who enlisted hoping to find their own
Glimpse of some distant dream that turned to be fatal.

To the many mothers still clinching their sorrow,
Dreading to hear one day the ringing of the phone,
May the Master of Love , your loved ones tomorrow,
Bring to you home safely, lest one day there'd be none.

Erjola

You're being tested baby,
Be strong and hang in there.
-Me, oh I'll be tested too
But only hope that like you
I am also strong…
Oh I'll be tested too
For He is just.
These are not meant
To make us faint.
They're not to prove
To Him a thing.
They render us strong
So when come along
Other dark and tormented seas
We will know how to maneuver,
Still float and love one another.
As I told you, my love, trust in your beloved Father
For the child who loves and serves Him, He permits but never
That he loses the graces of the many ordeals
That will have befallen him.
The almighty Science, the almighty Love, the almighty Wisdom
Who engineers it all for the good of the ones He favors.
Walk humbly with your Lord,
Fear deeply your dear God,
Love His Name endlessly.

Feeling down

Oh how dreadful it seems
The time spent all alone!
The hours one by one
Drag like in scary dreams.

You use all resources
From your spiritual safe,
Often open sources
To feed into your faith.

You call on the Father,
The One who delivers,
Hoping He will offer
Help to one who suffers.

But you are so distraught
That you cannot connect
And your disgruntled thoughts
Your prayer do affect.

So you lie all weary
Hoping the Almighty
Gives you of His power
To brighten your hour.

And until He replies,
Gives you His grace anew,
You cry and you despise
This aversion in you.

But be strong, you Christians,
Chosen of our dear Lord,
This reward has demands
And price you can afford.

Never has it been said
That the heavy ladden
Has had scorned his demand
Or been left unaided.

I brought you roses

I brought you roses, though perishable,
They are to many the most palpable
Of love expression.
I brought you roses because standing here,
I don't really know if you want to hear
Of my confusion.

I'd say I love you, of this you are sure
And though you respond with feelings so pure,
I know that you doubt of our tomorrow,
You were hurt again, still freh your sorrow.

If the Lord above decides to ignore
Or fails to bless us, for which I implore,
We will forever quarrel and depart
And after a while seek each other's heart.

Let us in pure wisdom be with one another
And give the final word to the Lord, our Savior.

Clearwater, 02/19/1999

There'll Come a Day

When God created man
He had for him a plan,
To leave his family
Take wife and then marry.
We failed to keep His laws
So in contempt we saw
All the wives and husbands
Fight to keep to their bands
The shine of that first day,
The glitz had gone away.

And sin entered the world
And misery unfurled.
So we repeatedly
Fail to keep faithfully
The law that is designed
To keep us well aligned
And save us from the craves,
Those for which our flesh raves.
Then we return and thirst
For what we lost at first.

So there will come a day,
My ship will come at bay,
And all of the sudden
I will find my maiden.
So on this blessed day
We will go far away
Free at last to enjoy
This grace He did deploy.
We will show to the rest
The Lord's divine kindness.

Appearances

From all the treasures of the world,
Gold, frankincense, platinum and pearl,
The Creator, the Redeemer,
When came time for Him to linger
On Earth and take our features,
Become like one of His creatures,
He wisely picked up poverty,
Known to us in great so many.

Desiring in us to instill,
His Love for all our hearts to fill,
He took the shape of her weak one,
Deprived of power from day one.
It was much too easy, He said,
To fear and love the ones ahead
For in this world societies
We always revere the mighties.

So when we ponder in our hearts
Reading His story part to part,
Within ourselves we slowly gain
This truth that should in us remain,
To love all the poors in this world,
Poor in health, knowledge, love and pearl
And keep this thought in us steady
That what you get isn't what you see.

You, The One I long For

You, the one I long for,
Long deep within the core
Can you feel its fierce pace
Missing your sweet embrace?

It throbs as to rejoice
At the sound of your voice,
Then ends in a flutter
When you leave thereafter.

I try so hard to quell
Its all quivering spell,
But the sound of your name
Makes it react the same.

This lovely sounding name
Within me seems to tame
My poor heart refusal
To love you, sweet Cantal.

So every word I say
Carries my mind away
And every thought that may
Pulsates my heart astray.

But for so many times
It answered to love chimes,
Some lovely, you could tell,
Others sounded like knell.

But for you, my jolie,
It wakes up suddenly.
Like the sun on my night,
You dissipate my fright.

You I long to embrace,
But who don't feel the pace
Of the beat of my heart,
Will you tear it apart?

Blesséd day

Oh blesséd be that day,
That day you crossed my path!
I can honestly say
I'm glad you're in my life.

The birds on my window
When they cuddle and coo
Say there's no more sorrow
For in my life there's you.

Who Are You

"Young lady, who are you,
Who are you anyway
That before I meet you
You're striking me this way?
While you're still far away, you're affecting my life,
What would become of me that day you cross my path?"

These are thoughts I ponder,
Chew over and over.
They leave me no answer
But to for you linger…

That was a short preview
Of my day without you,
But little do you know,
It's senseless to say so…
The truth is that instead,
You're up and down my head.

Letter to My Chantal

The more I think of you, the more I innovate,
You always find a way my soul to motivate.
I recall my mornings being dull and stagnant
Now with you on my mind things are so much different.
I must have told you so in many ways before,
Bear the redundancy, the non-ending encore.
See, it is the same heart palpitating for you,
And it is the same you; therefore the déjà vu.
So if I think of you and think I innovate,
Pardon the recurrence; I just can't help my fate.

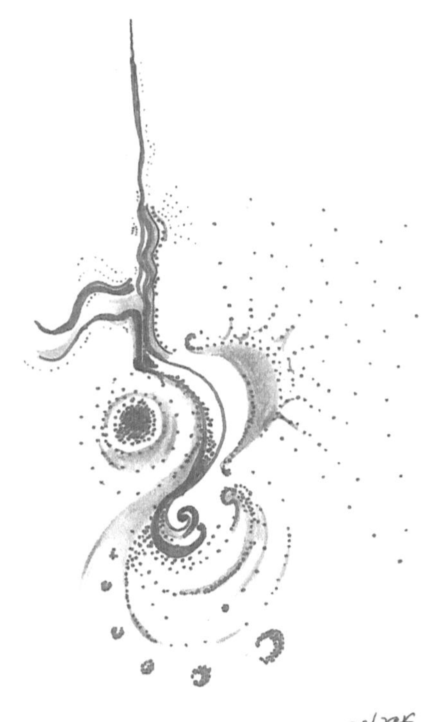

Days of Our Lives

There willl be days when I saw you
There will be days when I met you
There will be days when I had you
There will be days when I love you

There will be days I looked at you
There will be days not made for two
There will be days made for just you
And also days just for me too.

Then came the days of losing you,
Days so heart-wrenching for us two.
Then came the days I saw the true
Trophy you are; they were a slew.

There will be days empty and grue
There will be days I hated you.
There will be days, those were a few,
When others came to my rescue.

There will be days when I'll meet you
There will be days for me and you
There will be days I'll say "I do"
There'll be happy days for us two.

Faith Hope Love

He who believes, Father, tends also to give love.
Remember Lord, that love begets unfaltering hope.
This is the sole reason, alone in my alcove,
I kneel down before You to meditate and mope.

You are the Creator of every entity.
With Your breath You gave life to the whole galaxy.
This world should before You, in sheer humility,
Bow the head, bend the knee and beg for Your mercy.

I hope You cast upon Your servant's misery
And total submission some of Your clemency.
You alone, my dear God, can make my life anew
And from my emptiness show the world Your virtue.

Father how I adore Your divine tenderness.
You set this spark of love so deep within my heart
That every beat it strikes is only to witness
My love for You and from Your Face never depart.

Sheer Clemency

And so it goes, and so it goes
That in a world of foes
Always surges a friend,
A godsent of kindness and love
Who gives you gentle shoves,
And takes you to the end.

And so it goes, and so it goes
That the Almighty shows
His Mercy to His kids
And when you think that all is done
And every hope is gone
He shows His mighty deeds.

And so it goes, and so it goes,
I will follow you close,
My lovely guiding light.
For when you set your eyes on me,
Through blessed alchemy,
Ran out all my fright.

And so it goes, only God knows
The blessings HE bestows
Come down from His Mercy.
Just when I thought my life had passed
Just like a loving blast
His Power now all can see.

From The Heart

Lord in Your goodness,
Fill my emptiness.
Let my heart confess
To all Your knidness.

You love us, O Lord,
Gather us aboard
So we can afford
Your blessed reward.

For by Your power,
Divine Creator,
We will not falter
And lose our Savior.

Keep us dear Father,
In Your care ever,
And our hearts render
Faithful and fonder.

All our lives sustain,
Our hearts, please maintain
So that we remain
Within Your grace, plain.

This way at the end,
In Your great Heaven
We will notice then
The joys of Your plan.

For Christ is the light
Giving us insight
So Your children might
Remain in Your sight.

Father, Creator,
Jesus, Redeemer,
Spirit, Comforter,
Laud, praise forever!

To my sister, Jacotte

Belated Reproach

You could have chosen to live much longer
We had yet so much of feelings to share,
We had yet so much, being such a pair,
Of cozy late nights with good talk over.

You could have chosen to live much longer
But you chose instead as good pioneer,
To blaze other trails, to feel other fears,
When the inquiries became much stronger.

But you could have lived like the rest of us.
Carry little aches, bearing the crosses
That come to us from the Boss of bosses
And instill in us a much deeper trust.

You could have remained with no shady doubt
And we could have gone as we so long planned
To the old country care for the orphaned,
Bring about their smiles and erase their pouts.

You could have chosen to hang out longer
But then decided no more to be pair,
Leaving me the charge to pay just one fare
When will come my time to fly thereafter.

You could have chosen to be here with us
And not to force me to write down this song,
Knowing much too well how I can prolong
The many capers with old Morpheus.

Anytime Prayer

Standing before You,
My Lord and Savior,
We come beg a few
Of divine favors.

Just like You taught us
To pray the Father,
We pray Lord Jesus,
Be our sole Leader.

Whatever weakness'
Acted in Your Face
Our nature confess,
Rob us divine grace.

Unto You therefore
We put all our trust,
And humbly implore
That You make us just.

For only Your might,
O blesséd Savior
Will spare us the plight
Of those who prefer

To Your loving peace
The joys of this world
And therefore will miss
Heaven's golden pearl.

Standing before You,
My Lord and Savior,
Within us renew
Your Spirit power.

She'll Always Be My Little Baby

In desert lands my heart stranded.
In fields of hope, empty handed,
It longs for someone to color
The shade of gray of its pallor.
So deep inside it said to me:
"How I miss my little baby!"

And days went by so full of sun,
But golden rays it felt but none.
Rather withered, weary, loathsome,
It hoped for the day she would come,
Day of freedom, day of glory,
Day I'll see my little baby.

So finally, like Christmas time,
I saw her light, I heard her chime.
From that instant, sublime, tender,
For her it grew ever fonder.
Now it screams from deep within me:
"Please, please stay O little baby!"

Times shapes the lives it scopes over,
Leaving sorrow, leaving laughter.
But through its long, steady measure
We often get loving treasure
That brings us to say sincerely:
"She'll always be my lil' baby!"

Have Faith

So much I would like to tell you
But overload I should not do.
So I wrote you the following
To try to ease your sufferings.

It bothers me greatly
To see you so lovely
But yet made to carry
A burden so heavy.

Many times I ponder:
"Is it at all proper
With the feel I harbor
To nursing care for her?"

But I feel much compelled,
His Word should not be held.
Since all my fears they quell
Receive them dear, as well.

See, I read in the Book, the Lord reveal to us:
A woman will always suffer for her fetus,
Then after she gives birth, remember not her pain.
Her joy is much too great, and it's there to remain.

I heard you say to me
That you chose to empty
That deep well of mercy,
That faith we should carry.

But I see it this way, that while you've lost so much,
Even for your own sake, if I can say as such,
You should, but by no means, lose what is so precious,
That Force so powerful, that strong Hand of Jesus.

For He leads us, He says, have faith, I beg of you.
Trust blindly in His plan. When He sees that you do,
Mightily will unveil to you what He has planned.
But until then my dear, grab a hold of His Hand.

Saint John's Gospel

In the beginning was the Word
And the Word gladly was with God
And the Word, He, himself, was God!
And all things came to be through Him,
For nothing was made without Him.

What came to be through Him was life,
That life, Light of the human race,
That Light that shines in the dark strife,
That darkness just could not efface.

A man named John was sent from God.
He came to give testimony,
To testify so that many
Believe through Him in this great Light.
He was far from being the Light
But came only to testify
That the Light, source of every Life,
Into the world was due to come.
For the Light was into the world
And the world came to be through Him
But the world never knew of Him.

He came humbly amongst His own
But sadly, His Word, they disowned.
But to those who did accept Him
He gave power to be His kin,
Those who believe in His great Name,
Not born by flimsy human choice,
Nor by natural generation,
Nor by sole human decision
But only by the Will of God!

+

And the divine Word was made flesh
And amongst us He chose to dwell!
And all eyes witnessed His glory.
His glory as the Father's Son,
So full of Grace, so full of Truth!

John testified to Him and cried out saying:
"This is the One of whom I firmly attested
That though following me, He ranks ahead of me
Because He existed at all times, before me."

From His fullness we all received grace after grace.
The law was from Moses but through Jesus alone,
From His Father's mercy, we received Grace and Truth.
No one has ever seen the mighty Face of God.
The only Son of God, who's at the Father's side,
To the true believer, chooses to reveal Him.

Waiting For You

In the darkness of my bedroom
There I see shadow amid gloom.
I see forms fade with my blank eyes
But in my mind I see bright skies.

My heart fibers bleeding for you
Dictate my mind, ignite my soul.
The thoughts of you always brand new
Rush through my head. Can't sleep at all.

I think of time when we were us,
The things we did, the way we cared
For each other. Though so precious
Time did not spare the love we shared.

I think of things that could have been
Then I promise in life foreseen
To love you more each day I breathe
And kiss you at every sunrise.
I hope that you will not despise
The offer I will make that eve,
To change your name, make you my queen.

Immaculate Mary

All you faithful brethren come and let's admire
The Virgen now Mother, the daughter of David…
Come all, let's admire, clothed in white attire,
A wonder in herself, utmost creation bid.

She easily conceived with the help of no man,
Purest soul mesmerized by God's wonderful deeds.
Everyday her Spirit in deep prayers remain'
She rejoiced in her soul over all that God did:
She remains a virgin, with the most treasured Child.

She, the sweetest of doves, carries the strong Eagle,
The Ancient one, snow white, his praise loudly singing:
"My Son, You the richest, chose to come and mingle
In a wretched manger. You, the melodious String,
You remained all quiet, like a child so feeble,
Allow me, if you please, that for You, my voice rings."

"Your kingdom, O my Child, surpasses all others,
But You chose my poor womb as Your precious abode.
The heavens, Your glory, could not ever smother,
But You chose the meekest to make Your divine pod."

"Allow that Ezekiel come see You on my lap,
So he can recognize the One on the chariot
Carried by cherubims ..., today, You, my arms wrap.
And in a great tremor, sing in blessed riot:
Blessed be the splendor of the Place where You dwell!
But now You dwell in me, my womb is your abode,
The throne of Your great might, in my arms, softly held."

"Come see me, Isaiah, come see and let's rejoice,
See, now that I conceived although a virgin still,
Prophet of the Spirit, with visions of best choice,
Behold Emmanuel whom you could only feel..."

"So come all you faithful, driven by the Spirit,
You who deep in your heart feel the warmth of his Love...
Stand up; give praise out loud, on bended knees, come meet,
Held gently in my arms, is the Bread from above."

In Deepest Sympathy

There is always a better way
To see the pain you feel today.
While you're thinking she's gone away,
Think of the gain that came her way.

She carried that body so long,
Never complained, was always strong.
Her misery not to prolong
God, his angels, put her among.

Let Christmas be merry

Let there be a merry Christmas
Despite the turmoil in our world!
Let there be a merry Christmas
With warm manger and golden pearls.

Let there be a merry Christmas,
This marvel beyond all telling
That the good Lord from ages past
Sent all His prophet heralding.

Let there be a merry Christmas,
For deep within our infancy
This Gift bestowed was meant to last
Throughout our life, from God's mercy.

Let there be a merry Christmas
For God almighty chose to wear
Just for our sake a form that pass'
So, to be His children, we'd dare.

Let there be a merry Christmas,
There'll never be another one.
Beware that the next time He pass'
Of His graces you'd come undone.

For the next time He comes around
He will not be small, shivering.
With His army and blasting sound
He'll come for some serious sieving.

Let there be a merry Christmas
And make it last the whole year through
So that next time the trumpet blasts
You'd be given a life brand new.

Dreadful Way Home

Varied are the channels, the Lord in his wisdom,
Remind His children of the way to His kingdom.
For neither the hour, the time, nor circomstance
Can we know when to make before God our entrance.

On any given day, if they see the sunrise,
Great many among us face up with some surprise.
It's never expected and can be unpleasant
For never departure has been known to enchant.

So this early morning, with a light overcast,
All went on as usual around him. Not a blast.
Light breakfast, shower, shave then up to work he went,
And all he could think of was how to make the rent.

See, business had been slow. No help came from the rain
Which chose to fall so much backing up the main drain.
People had to stay home, it was more than a choice
From fear of getting soaked, fall sick and lose their voice.

This early spring has been a tad too wet for him,
It was way too early for May flower to gleam.
He deemed it was senseless for nature to downpour
So much water to change the Earth face and contour.

He walked to the kiosk, got the news he prefers,
Saw the headlines and said: "Oh wow! I so differ"!
And then he shook his head, headed for the subway,
Part of this long routine leading to work each day.

He met the neighbor's wife. They then chatted briefly.
She stopped at the cleaners, they parted there vaguely.
The sun peeped a short while, twas not gusting today,
Yesterday was a mess, the winds on us all preyed.

He went with peppy steps crossing the street corners,
Waving at passersby, familiar store owners,
Nothing seems unusual as he stepped in to buy
Black coffee and bagel at the deli Bed-Stuy.

With the deli owner after exchanging jokes,
He stepped back in the street, set for the daily pokes
A subway rider gets from other commuters.
Nothing to gripe about, just keep tight your shutters.

As he reached the stairway a crowd was exiting.
So he stood patiently but was shoved, weirdest thing,
By some guy in some rush, or some much heated chase,
The hot coffee he held spilled on pants and briefcase.

So there he stood half wet with onlookers around
Who like everybody were all rushing work bound.
Funny how small hazards can come as forewarning,
As we go on living and their message shunning!

As he stood, came roaring the train uptown express,
Feeling wet, cold, wishing he could somehow undress,
Lost in the crowd, thoughts on his now wet and cold slacks,
There came the fatal shove. He felt down in the tracks.